Writers Inspiring Writers

What I

Wish

I'd Known

EDITED BY

New York Times Bestselling Author

Jennifer Probst
&
Erin Branscom

Cover design by Hang Le
Interior Format by The Killion Group, Inc.

ISBN: 979-8-88662-007-8 Paperback
ISBN: 979-8-88662-006-1 Digital

DEDICATION

Dedicated to every author who has been a guest on the *Meet the Author Show* on Amazon Live, as well as future guests. Thank you for sharing your beautiful books with the world. Your words, encouragement, and appearances encourage the rest of us. We appreciate you so much.
  ~ *Erin*

For every new writer who ever questioned if they were alone and dreamed of receiving not only guidance, but reassurance, this is for you. Welcome to the tribe. We got you.

For all the author-contributors in this book who took their precious time and energy to share their words, thank you. I believe you've made a difference.
  ~ *Jen*

TABLE OF CONTENTS

Introduction

INTRODUCTION

Jennifer Probst & Erin Branscom

WRITING IS HARD.

Not only the craft, but the entire lifestyle. It's a career that so many feel passionate about: Writing offers a place to pour our creative soul and show a unique perspective on the world, but it's also filled with long days alone in a room and blank pages that sometimes taunt and torture with possibilities, rejections, poor sales, overwhelming marketing and PR tasks, and daunting author communities and social media.

Like any career, mentors help guide us. Speaking personally with an author you admire can help bolster motivation and sharpen clarity in our own work. Beginning writers dream of gathering as much knowledge as possible from bestselling, career authors in order to help their own journey.

What if you could gather these experts in a room together and ask them about their critical advice in launching and sustaining a successful writing career?

Wouldn't that knowledge be priceless?

That is the goal of this book: To reach far

and wide, and share advice these writers would have told their younger self.

We are no longer living in a world where information is kept greedily. The more information shared, the more we can offer a helping hand to the ones beginning—the ones that reflect who we were when we began attacking that first blank page.

Within these pages, we've brought together authors who reflect the wide range of books found on the shelves. Each one has written a personal essay addressing this question: *What do I wish I had known when I was starting out?* They've not only given freely of their precious time from their own writing, they've reached deep to truly analyze the question and offer something unique.

In a way, this is their book, not ours. Our dream was to gather up the information and bring it to you in a format that can be read easily, savored, analyzed, and used over and over again. It's a book you can keep coming back to as your writing career grows and changes.

It's a book about giving back to the author community.

It's been an honor for us to work with these authors and hear their stories.

THE SECRET SAUCE

Jennifer Probst

WHEN I WAS a new writer, I revered established authors. I looked at them as members of a secret club that I fantasized about entering daily. Of course, back in the old days, there was no real contact with published authors, so it was more of a dream. Today, we get to meet our favorite writers on a consistent basis—whether on social media, at signings, or at conferences.

I always dreamed of asking published authors for their best advice. Advice on how to write, market, create amazing books like they did, and avoid making mistakes. Advice on how to make money, get an agent, get published, and sign good contracts.

If I could tap into their brain and funnel all of their knowledge from years of writing, I figured it would be so much easier. If I could immerse myself in learning what to do and what not to do, it would make my career flourish. It may make me famous. It may make me rich.

Will this book guarantee you all of these things?

No. Because unfortunately, my dear writers, that is something you must do on your own, following the unique path only you can.

So, then, why would you read this book?

Because, within these pages, you will find a fountain of counsel from authors who have not only been multi-published, but who have a solid fanbase. Authors who have hit the bestseller lists. Authors who have walked this road before, and emerged with new information, insights, and practical tips they wish they'd known first starting out.

If there is one absolute fact and guarantee I can make after writing steadily for over thirty years, and penning over fifty novels, novellas, short stories, essays, and poems, it's this:

There is no secret sauce.

Being a writer is a mysterious, magical, awful, terrible, joyous career. I've learned to revel in both the good and bad, the ups and downs; because like life, you can't have one without the other. If there weren't difficult books that made you work and sweat, you'd never truly appreciate the ones that are gifts.

What I can offer are the exact things I'd tell my twelve year-old self who was beginning on this long writing journey. What I'd whisper in my thirty- and forty-two year-old ear when things got really bad, and then when things got really good. What I'd tell myself two years ago when the world fell apart and, like most authors, I needed to pivot.

My own secret sauce is quite simple, but it's the simple words that, I believe, mean the most.

1. Don't let anyone else try to tell you about your talent, your dreams, your plans, or what to do about your writing.

No one. Not a beloved spouse or grandmother, or well-meaning child or friend. Because while these people may have the best intentions, it is not their life and it is not their business what you choose to write, for whom you choose to write, and how you decide to go about sharing your work with the world.

Young writers want so badly to be published. I signed some terrible contracts in my pursuit of publication. I'd tell the following to that eager girl who decided no one else would ever buy her work and this opportunity was the *only one* to hang on: In a decade, the world would be knocking on her door. Read everything before you sign. Hire a literary lawyer if you don't have an agent. Value your work, because no one else will.

I had a high school English teacher tell me it would be best not to think I'd be a full time writer. I had so-called friends laugh and tease me about my pursuit because, after years, I wasn't making a penny from it.

I was counseled on getting a second "real" job to make money, and told it was a cute hobby. I was also informed my writing was what prevented me from meeting a nice guy and settling down into a "real" life.

But that girl dreamed hot and bright and knew in her gut that one day her words would be published. With self-publishing, it's much easier to do it without gatekeepers, but you still must treat the work with reverence and as a business, not a hobby.

Unless it is a hobby. That's fine—but if you want to be a career author, as I think many of you do, it begins in the mind first. Treating your writing like a business is key. Keeping yourself accountable is important. That's how real progress is made.

And when you're staring down the barrel of 100,000 words and a blank page, you will need all that business training to keep going. Every word counts. Every word gets you farther—and I'd tell that girl to not discount one poem, short story, or journal entry because all writing is critical and leads to finished, published stories.

Be responsible for your career and your choices. Block out the naysayers. It's easy to judge someone else's life, isn't it? Remember to go back to the words when you get lost. Find your story. Believe in yourself. This is critical to success.

2. There are no wrong paths: Only choices.

Don't worry that one bad book, contract, or marketing mishap will ruin your career. Don't worry that if you miss that deadline or have to push a book or deadline out because of emergencies or burnout that it will destroy everything you've built. It's simply not true.

Looking back, I will never regret not writing another book. I'd regret time not spent with my family, my kids, or taking space for self-care, because energy keeps my butt in the chair and my mind sharp with creative ideas.

Restart: In my darkest days, I believed I could never come back and that I'd never be able to write again. This never happened. Eventually, I came back to the story, even if it was longer than I expected. Some books need more cooking time, some need longer edits, and some just don't ever bloom from the seed of a good idea to a fleshed-out manuscript. If you miss a writing day and are behind, don't waste time berating yourself. Restart. Every day is a new beginning and no time is wasted. You need to make mistakes to thrive, because it forces you to grow. Don't be afraid of mistakes—do your research, listen to your gut, trust your creative Muse, and it will all be okay.

3. Protect the work.

I talked about this at length in *Write Naked*. When you create something, there will be a long line of people who will judge your work. This is part of the contract signed when you are brave enough to show your heart and soul to the world. The ones who judge harshly may be the exact ones who have been too afraid to expose their own art. How you deal with this judgment can affect your psyche and send your poor battered Muse into hiding.

Every rejection gave me thick skin and a passion to keep going, but reviews were harder for me to shake off. Many times I'd try to write and hear the harsh words in my head until I couldn't create anything new. I learned with experience, time, and advice from others that my job was to block out the noise of the world around me and tell my story. To believe in myself and my purpose and my writing. I finally understood not everyone was going to like what I put out, and that is okay. More than okay: This is what makes art awe-inspiring—the broad range of variety.

How could we possibly believe everyone will like one voice, thought, or perspective?

Learn how to protect the work. Keep it close and cherished. Shake it off. Call a supportive friend and rage about unfairness. Do what you need to get rid of the negativity and go back to work.

If you learn this skill, you can have a healthier, happier career in writing.

That's it. The secret sauce. No, it won't help you hit the bestseller list, get a movie deal, or be a book club pick.

But that's not as important as showing up daily, doing the work, avoiding burnout, and being happy about what you choose to do with your writing. Because when you hit that stride, and realize this is what you were meant to do?

You've found yourself. And that will give you so much more than fame or kudos or money.

May the words be with you, always.

Jennifer Probst

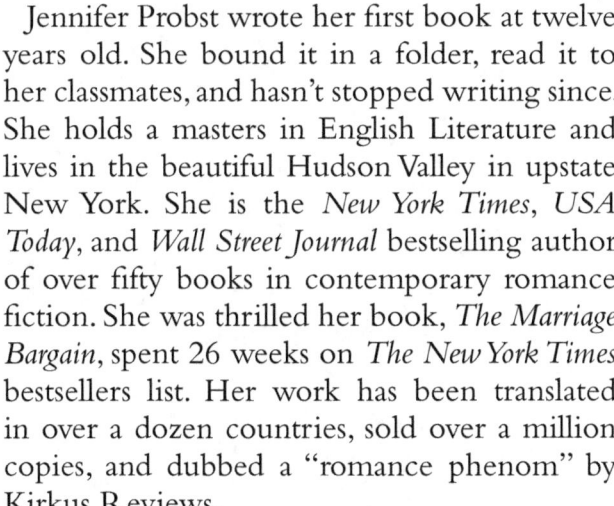

Jennifer Probst wrote her first book at twelve years old. She bound it in a folder, read it to her classmates, and hasn't stopped writing since. She holds a masters in English Literature and lives in the beautiful Hudson Valley in upstate New York. She is the *New York Times*, *USA Today*, and *Wall Street Journal* bestselling author of over fifty books in contemporary romance fiction. She was thrilled her book, *The Marriage Bargain*, spent 26 weeks on *The New York Times* bestsellers list. Her work has been translated in over a dozen countries, sold over a million copies, and dubbed a "romance phenom" by Kirkus Reviews.

Website: www.jenniferprobst.com/

Instagram: www.instagram.com/
authorjenniferprobst/

Facebook: www.facebook.com/jenniferprobst.
authorpage/

Grab my nonfiction work for authors—
Write Naked and Write True—on my website.

Write Naked (jenniferprobst.com)
Write True (jenniferprobst.com)

NEED MOTIVATION? FOCUS ON THE PERSON WHO NEEDS YOUR STORY

Eden Appiah-Kubi

THERE'S A GREAT quote from Toni Morrison that hopefully every writer has heard: "If there's a book that you want to read, but it hasn't been written yet, then you must write it." Honestly, I don't think I've heard better motivation for writing before or since. It points out two true things in one powerful sentence: 1) A love of writing comes from a love of reading and stories. 2) Even though it feels like everything has been done, everyone's story hasn't been told yet. Still, these words—powerful as they are—may not be enough to keep you going until the very last page. For that, let me offer this corollary to the wise advice above: "There is someone out there who needs that book that you must write. To keep writing, focus on them."

When I started writing *The Bennet Women*, I was working in an indie book shop in Washington, D.C. Between shelving books, checking out customers, and our frequent author talks, I saw a lot of books—and few people with my story. This was the Bush era, and even though it wasn't long ago, it was difficult to find books with Black protagonists set in contemporary times; and *very* hard to find books that were not wholly or mostly about how the Black character was contending with racism. Also, despite the early aughts being the age of chick lit, I can't recall ever seeing a book with a Black heroine older than 18 or younger than 35. If you had looked at the shelves of our bookstore, someone like me simply didn't exist.

I was waiting for a novel that centered on a young, nerdy Black woman—before Issa Rae, there was some unspoken rule that Black protagonists were supposed to be cool— or at least, not uncool. (In reality we can be everything, including *huge dorks*.) When the inspiration for *The Bennet Women* struck, I knew I couldn't keep waiting for another author to write this story. I knew who EJ was, I knew her diverse circle of friends, I knew her arrogant Asian-American love interest: It was up to me to get it all down.

But before I had the idea for the story, I had the yearning for it. I bought and treasured anything that remotely resembled it: The dark-skinned heroine with her Asian-American love interest in Nicola Yoon's *The Sun Is Also a Star*; the curvy, ambitious heroine with her diverse circle of friends in Jasmine Guillory's *The Wedding Date*; the witty banter between the heroine and her romantic lead who has to change for the better in Talia Hibbert's *The Princess Trap*. These are just a few of the many stories I grabbed with both hands as soon as I was aware of their existence. The thing that kept me going when I was just sick to death of my own typos was the idea that someone would see my book on a shelf and think, "Finally, this is for me."

I speak from a Black woman's perspective because that's what I am, but I'm also a reader who goes to books looking for windows and mirrors. Before I left high school, I read Jane Austen, Armistead Maupin, Amy Tan, and Sandra Cisneros. Whether I was reading for school or for pleasure, there was always something in the text that helped me feel more connected to the human experience. So if you write about friendship, finding courage, triumphing over adversity, or the simple beauty of a quiet life, someone needs to hear it. Someone needs you to write it. And if you're a Black person, an indigenous person, a woman of color, and/or part of the LGBTQIA community, someone has been waiting for your perspective for a long time.

Whether you're traditionally published, self-published, or throwing your story up on the internet and hoping for the best, once something you write is out in the world, you have no control over how it will be received (culturally or commercially). Focusing on the people who need your story keeps you from trying to do the impossible: Writing to please everyone. Also, should you ever get traditionally published, remembering who you're writing for can be a light through the choppy waters of rewrites, compromise, and frustration. On the other side of publication, remembering who you wrote the book for can help give you the energy for interviews, as well as the courage to do things out of your comfort zone—like joining TikTok. When what you're doing is in the name of reaching your readers, the effort suddenly becomes worthwhile.

But we're getting ahead of ourselves. Writing can be a marathon without a map (especially for pantsers like me). I got the idea for my novel, *The Bennet Women*, in 2007. I didn't work seriously on it until 2011, and it took me five years to complete my first manuscript. Even if you write faster than that, editing feels like it takes years. When you're in the middle of killing your darlings, proofreading, or removing every instance of the word "just" from your manuscript, you're going to need some motivation to keep going. That motivation is the reader who's waiting for your book. You have something to say that they need to hear. Get going.

Eden Appiah-Kubi is the author of the Austen-inspired contemporary romance, *The Bennet Women*. She loves writing about Black nerdy heroines falling in love. A former Peace

Corps volunteer, today she lives about 10 minutes from where she grew up in the D.C. suburbs of Maryland with her husband and hilarious daughter.

Website: www.Edenawrites.com

Instagram: www.instagram.com/edenawrites/

TikTok: www.tiktok.com/t/ZTR2kECX4/

Facebook: https://m.facebook.com/
EdenAWrites

WRITER'S LIFE RUINED MY LIFE

Skye McDonald

BEFORE WRITING TOOK hold of my brain, I had it all figured out. I knew what adulting was supposed to look like. What "fun" and "busy" and "distracted" all meant. Then along came characters who whispered inside my head (if you're a writer, you get that this is normal, not madness), and everything flipped over.

I don't blame the long hours immersed in my Anti-Belle series, the whirlwind of new friends and fellow authors on Twitter, or the agony of being out on submission. None of those elements of becoming an author ended my marriage or my teaching career. But they all combined to upend my previously stable, steady routine.

This is not a cautionary tale, however. I do not mean to suggest the same will happen to you. Nothing falls apart that wasn't ready to be deconstructed. Becoming an author made me see the world differently. My new point-of-view helped me realize that I didn't have life all figured out. Suddenly, I was willing to do a little editing of my own story.

So while *ruined* may be harsh, it's fair to say that becoming a published author taught me many lessons about myself, my goals, and what I truly wanted.

Writing began as a hobby that grew into an obsession until, finally, I had written an entire series. For years, I lived half in reality and half in the world of the Anti-Belles. Teaching sci-fi to high schoolers and daydreaming about steamy love stories was a tricky tightrope to walk. When at last I was ready to let others see my work, I began to build my social media platform. That brought me friends and peers to commiserate with. It also gave me even more of an escape from my day-to-day.

I decided to query *Not Suitable for Work*. Writing had been a hobby long enough. I got an agent through a non-traditional pitch letter wherein I pitched the whole series, not just my first book. We set about editing *NSFW* together. I was over the moon as we went out on submission.

It was around then that my marriage fell apart.

This isn't a sob story. He and I are the best of friends now, although we certainly weren't then. But becoming Skye McDonald, romance novelist, drove a wedge between us that couldn't be ignored. So, as my book was sent to publisher after publisher, I went on a soul journey to discover who I was—and a separation to determine who we wanted to be.

Not Suitable for Work was out on submission for a year. In that time, my marriage officially ended. I hurt and cried a lot, both for the personal upheaval and the litany of publisher responses that said, "Good book, but no thanks." I tried to understand how my book could be good and yet unwanted. I tried to figure out who the heck I'd become, and why everything was so damn hard all of a sudden.

Over a year later, I had to admit that the hunt for a traditional publisher was at a dead end. After all the personal turmoil, this knowledge cut deep. I had a choice: Shelve my beloved series or make a final push to get it out into the world on my own.

The person I was dating at the time offered me heartfelt words that I'll never forget: "Ten years from now, are you going to regret not giving your books one final shot?"

I knew the answer. And so, I created a sole proprietorship for Anti-Belle Books and published *Not Suitable for Work*. Then, I published *Off the Record* and *Nemesis*.

And then!

I joined forces with my "Quick & Dirty Romance Podcast" bestie, Sarah Smith, and Anti-Belle Books began to publish Sarah Skye's Unlikely Pairings series. There are more books to come, as well as a bigger project my press is working on. But all that to say, my dream of becoming an author has manifested. It just took a different route than I expected.

Through it all, I made amends and found common ground with my ex-husband. I broke up with the guy who gave me those inspirational words and moved on. I wrapped up my teaching career and kicked off my dream of becoming a personal trainer and coach.

I kept editing and revising my own life. In writing and in reality, I keep living, hurting, and hoping. Inspiration and joy are part of my days *and* my stories.

The Writer's Life means different things to different people. Sometimes it's a passion project. Sometimes it's an aspiring career. And sometimes, completely out of nowhere, it's the catalyst you need to make fundamental change. It's humility and heartache and hope all in one. It's triumph, and pride, and dismay, and tears, and laughter, and all the swooning.

But no matter what it is, it's you.

It's your life, poured out in a story. It's your dreams, put down for the world—or for no one but you—to see. It's your journey. Your goal. Your lesson to learn.

The Writer's Life is as unique as each brilliant individual who dares to put their thoughts on a page. If I learned anything by becoming a writer, it's that.

So, yes, the Writer's Life ruined my life, but not really. Because my life is now so much richer and fuller as a result. If I had to go and do it again, I'd surely edit a few lines. But I definitely wouldn't change the plot.

Skye McDonald's Anti-Belle series features Nashville women learning to love themselves before they can claim their happily-ever-after. Skye also co-authors the Unlikely Pairings novels with Sarah Smith, writing as Sarah Skye. She is also a personal development coach, helping women to become the heroes of their own stories via fitness, habit changes, and self-love.

Skye lives in Montclair, NJ. In her free time, she hikes with her dog, runs Spartan races, travels, scuba dives, and runs. Someday she'll take a break and chill out, preferably on a beach. But not yet. There's so much life to live first.

Website: www.authorskyemcdonald.com

Instagram: www.instagram.com/
writerskyemcd

Read:
Anti-Belle Series Anti-Belle (3 book series)
Kindle Edition (amazon.com)

WHAT I WISH I'D DONE DIFFERENTLY ...

Samantha Young

IT WAS 2011 and self-publishing was at the beginning of its exciting evolution via Amazon's Kindle Direct Publishing (KDP). Social media, as it is now, was a key medium in which to market these books I'd spent years writing. I focused my attention mostly on reaching out to book bloggers but also on building my social media platforms. Facebook was my biggest avenue for reaching new readers, and the algorithms were entirely different back then. When *On Dublin Street,* my first adult contemporary romance, reached number one in the U.S. on Amazon, my Facebook page flooded with new followers. Suddenly I went from around ten thousand followers to seventy thousand followers. The beauty of it was that this was a period before Facebook launched its ad platform, so they weren't hiding business page posts in order to force businesses into spending to reach more users.

So, I focused on social media, and I neglected

my newsletter. I had the subscribe button on my website and the link in the back of all my books, but I wasn't actively working to build my newsletter base. It took me too long to realize just how important a newsletter was because I felt secure in the fact that I had so many followers on my social media pages. And when the Facebook ads platform was introduced, the size of my page allowed me to create great targeted ads.

However, as the market has grown more saturated, reaching audiences has also grown more difficult. As my peers began working on newsletter-building promotions, I watched as their preorders increased, as their release days resulted in high ranks and greater sales. Moving my focus to my newsletter has had quite a significant impact. My sales have increased again and my audience continues to grow far more exponentially than it did in the lull between *On Dublin Street*'s success and my books after that series finished.

What frustrates me, though, is that if I'd capitalized on that series' success when it was at its height, if I'd focused on my newsletter when *On Dublin Street* first released, my newsletter would be phenomenally reader strong. It's one of my regrets, and I tell all new authors that building your newsletter is more important than you can ever know. If the last decade in publishing has proven anything, it's that authors cannot rely on social media platforms alone. While they are imperative for reaching current and new readers and for building sales, it's also risky to rely solely on them. Not only are these platforms continually evolving in ways where their developments can impact negatively the businesses using them, I've also seen technical glitches wipe out an author's entire profile and page they've spent years building.

A strong newsletter means having the ability to reach your core readership without worrying so much that a change might mean the difference between your book news reaching thousands of readers and only reaching a handful. While nothing is one hundred percent guaranteed in this industry, a newsletter is a far more stable and secure way to stay connected to your growing readership.

Samantha Young is a *New York Times*, *USA Today* and *Wall Street Journal* bestselling author from Scotland. She's been nominated for several Goodreads Choice Awards. She writes adult contemporary and paranormal romance, young adult urban fantasy, and younger contemporary fiction. Currently published in 31 countries, Samantha is a number-one international-bestselling author.

Website: www.authorsamanthayoung.com

Facebook: www.facebook.com/
AuthorSamanthaYoung

Instagram: www.instagram.com/
authorsamanthayoung/

TikTok: @authorsamanthayoung

Read:
Here With Me (The Adair Family Series #1)

Buy:
books2read.com/herewithme

*I came to Scotland to make peace with the past and
instead found scandal, danger... and him.*

FOR THE LOVE OF WRITING

Samantha Chase

I FELL IN LOVE with writing when I was eight years old.

I hand-wrote my first romance novel when I was 15.

I didn't publish my first book until I was 43.

Technically, I was a late-bloomer in this business, but once I got started, it was like every story I ever thought of writing started clamoring to get out.

A little background on me: I didn't go to school for journalism or even anything related to it. I dropped out of college after a year and a half, got married at 22, and had a baby at 23. We lived paycheck to paycheck (barely) and I had a second child when I was 31. We lived in a super small house—896 square feet—and with four of us, there was barely any room for anything other than the basics. But once I decided that I really wanted to write, we made things work.

I had a desk in the corner of our little dining room and I would sit at that as often as I could—after dinner, during my lunch breaks (I lived close to the office at the time and would come home to eat)—and if the noise level of being smack-dab in the middle of the house got to be too much, I'd sit on my bed with the door closed and write some more.

I also might have written some while sitting in my cubicle at work …

Either way, I wrote.

A lot.

Every spare moment I could find, I made myself sit down and get the words out.

I self-published my first book in November of 2011. I had received 19 rejections and came to the realization that I do *not* handle rejection well. I was teaching creative writing to homeschoolers at the time and my students were the ones who introduced me to self-publishing. I was completely oblivious to how to do any of it and one of my students even made my first book cover for me! I hit publish and waited.

And waited.

And waited.

I knew nothing about all that went into being an indie author and that I actually had to market and promote and have a social media presence … so basically, that book sold around 30 copies that first year. But I kept writing. I had a binder of about two dozen works-in-progress and couldn't find a story that was really sticking with me, but in November of 2012, I did National Novel Writing Month and made myself sit and do those 50,000 words. I wrote a Christmas romance in eleven days and really fell in love with the story. I decided to self-publish it as a way to keep my name out there until I wrote a longer book. The plan was to put it out for free, but Amazon didn't allow that and I had to do it for 99 cents.

It sold 10,000 copies that first month (knowing only a little bit more about marketing and promoting at that point) and that's when I knew that I needed to build on that success.

I reasoned with myself that if I could write 50,000 words in a matter of weeks, then I could put out a book a month and potentially quit the office job that I hated and finally have my dream career! So again, I sat at that desk in the corner, my family got used to seeing me from the back only every night, and I wrote like mad. In 2013, I published ten books and started getting more comfortable with everything I needed to do on my own to keep going.

Word of advice: Don't try to write ten books in a year. It's exhausting.

Still, I kept going. I networked and got involved in cross-promoting and then was invited to participate in a box set where all the heroes were CEOs. It seemed like a fun project and I was excited to even be asked. In the meantime, my income from writing far surpassed my income from my office job and my husband and I sat down and talked about me quitting my office job and being a full-time author. It was super scary because my office job had income security. One bad book could hurt us. I convinced him to let me take this leap of faith and I gave my two-week notice.

The best part of it? On my last day at that job, the box set hit the *New York Times* bestseller's list!

That's when I knew I was making the right choice.

But I certainly didn't relax.

I miss relaxing ...

And the thing is, I still kept going. I was diligent in making myself write, I kept learning about the business, I kept networking. By 2014, I had an agent and within three months, I had my first traditional publishing contract.

Our lives changed drastically after that.

We moved out of our 896 square-foot house and bought a house three times as large that had an office for me! A real office! Not my bed, not the corner of the dining room, but a room that is all mine and filled with books that I've written, things that inspire me, things readers have sent to me, and a whole lot of stuff that simply makes me smile.

And a snoring pug because she believes she's part of the creative process.

I've now published 87 books and by the end of 2022, I will have published a total of 92.

I'm not as disciplined as I used to be, but I'm also not trying to put out ten books a year. My goal is around seven and I am very consistent with my release schedule. I just celebrated my ten-year publishing anniversary and I cannot believe how blessed I am.

You're never too old to chase your dream and achieve it. I'm proof of that.

Samantha Chase is a *New York Times* and *USA Today* bestseller of contemporary romance that's hotter than sweet, sweeter than hot. She released her debut novel in 2011 and currently has more than 80 titles under her belt— including *The Christmas Cottage*, which was a Hallmark Christmas movie in 2017! She's a Disney enthusiast who still happily listens to 80s rock. When she's not working on a new story, she spends her time reading romances, playing way too many games of solitaire on Facebook, wearing a tiara while playing with her sassy pug Maylene … oh, and spending time with her husband of 32 years and their two sons in Wake Forest, North Carolina.

Sign up for my mailing list and get exclusive content and chances to win members-only prizes! www.chasing-romance.com/newsletter

<u>Start a fun new small town romance series:</u> www.chasing-romance.com/the-donovans-series

<u>Where to Find Me:</u>

Website: www.chasing-romance.com

Facebook: www.facebook.com/
SamanthaChaseFanClub

Instagram: www.instagram.com/
samanthachaseromance/

Twitter: https://twitter.com/SamanthaChase3

Reader Group: www.facebook.com/
groups/1034673493228089/

A LETTER FROM PRESENT ME

K Webster

IF PRESENT ME could send an email to Past Me, I'd have quite a few things to say to that completely clueless newbie author. In fact, I'd probably have a 500-page essay detailing everything I need Past Me to know about Present Me. Luckily, if you're just starting out, you'll get the condensed version. This is the main gist in a nutshell:

Make the most of everything you have now, rather than always jumping onto what's coming next.

What does that mean?

When I started out, I immediately climbed onto the hamster wheel. I set a breakneck pace for myself where I equated success to the number of books I could release. In all fairness, my numbers were there. Each time I'd release, I'd have a burst of new money from my new books. It felt as though if I could release more, I'd make more.

And I totally nailed it. I was making good money spinning all my plates in the air at once.

Until I dropped my first plate. When you're doing all the things, all the time, all at once, you're bound to slip up. The past couple of years—since the pandemic began—have been hard on everyone and our lives have been turned upside down. For me, the pandemic triggered a series of events that forced me to take a hard look at my author business and how I was growing it. There was no way I'd be able to sustain the pace I'd set for myself. My health was deteriorating along with my sanity.

But, I still needed money.

Something had to give. Releasing every month, and sometimes twice a month, wasn't possible anymore. I still needed to earn a good income, but it was time to get creative about how that would come about.

I spent that last year digging in and learning more about marketing, improving my newsletters, and a whole pile of other things to "nurture my backlist." It was triggered by what an author, Alana Albertson, said to me. She said, "I was tired of being a frontlist author. I wanted to be a backlist author."

That statement was just the thump on the head I needed. I'd spent nearly a decade writing and publishing books. There was an entire library of books I never mentioned or posted about, some I even forgot I wrote, and some that collected dust because it was "an old book no one will care about."

I was a frontlist, hamster-wheel running, book-publishing spaz. But, I had over a hundred books in my backlist that could be working for me. Books I'd already worked hard on and invested in. Why wasn't I leading readers to all those books?

Sure, the next book is exciting and it keeps momentum going, but there were so many ways I could breathe life into old books, if I'd just take the time to do so.

So, I did.

I worked on new covers, updated frontmatter and backmatter, combined books to make box sets, created special editions, started spotlighting older books in my newsletter, and so on. The point is, I made a plan of attack. I took a few books at a time and breathed new life into them. Our books are investments that will continue to pay us over time. We just have to freshen them up every now and again to present them to our audiences in new, eye-catching ways. It's worth the trouble and time, I assure you.

In the summer of 2021, one of my books that was five-and-a-half years old at the time went viral on TikTok. That one book sold more than 60,000 copies that month. Luckily, I'd just given it a new cover, raised the price, and came up with a new blurb. I'd had the front and backmatter updated, too. I believed that by taking the time to give it a fresh look, it was ready to catch fire … and it did. Since that book took off, it has continually outperformed all my other books (including new releases) since then. The proof was in the pudding!

If you're just starting out, there are ways to give one book multiple different ways of getting seen. Special or alternate covers are an easy marketing tool, as readers love collecting them. Sometimes it's as simple as skimming through your book and coming up with some new teasers that look different than what you've done before. Additionally, you could spend some time making TikTok videos or spotlighting the book in your newsletter. By thinking up various ways to shine light on an older book you've already done the hard work for, you'll no doubt reap the financial rewards.

Don't be like Past Me who was go, go, go. Be like Present Me: Stop and smell the roses (or your old books in this case) and remember what made them so special in the first place. Tap into that and capitalize on it.

You've got this.

I believe in you.

K Webster is a *USA Today* bestselling author. Her titles have claimed many bestseller tags in numerous categories, are translated in multiple languages, and have been adapted into audiobooks. She lives in "Tornado Alley" with her husband, two children, and her baby dog named Blue. When she's not writing, she's reading, drinking copious amounts of coffee, and researching aliens.

Website: www.authorkwebster.com/

Instagram:www.instagram.com/
authorkwebster/

Facebook:www.facebook.com/
authorkwebster

Tiktok: www.tiktok.com/@authorkwebster

Twitter: https://twitter.com/KristiWebster

BEING YOU

Jody Holford (Sophie Sullivan)

BEING A WRITER is a lot like being in high school: You know, deep down, that everyone feels the same way and has similar experiences, but when you glance up through lowered lashes to take a quick peek, it seems like others are navigating the terrain so much better than you. Usually, in cooler clothes. It is really hard not to fall down a rabbit hole, wondering how you can pull off *their* look, *their* style, *their* success. The truth is, you aren't them, so you can't. It took me quite a while to realize that this is a gift. The stories I give to the world are my own and no one can tell them quite like I do. The same is true for you. I'll repeat: That is a gift.

It is all too easy to wish or wonder about other paths and I've spent a lot of time doing just that. What I've realized is, this takes me away from the thing that brings me joy: the writing. For me, and I'm betting for many others, not comparing myself to the cool kids is really hard to do. I've published more than 25 books, in three genres, under two names. I still question whether or not I've "made it."

It's hard not to get caught up in what that really means and "making it" is different for everyone. It helps me to define success for myself. When I signed my deal with St. Martin's Press, I wrote myself a note that said: *This is what I've worked for, waited for, and been wanting. I am happy and content in this moment.* I look back at this note when I'm feeling unsure of my own path, wondering if I should have veered off at that last fork in the road. It's a reminder that I'm doing what I set out to do. I highly recommend you do this for yourself. There will be many days when you need it to recenter and refocus yourself.

If I go back to the high school analogy, social media is the hallway during break time. It's loud, distracting, and anxiety inducing. But it's also a nice … well, break. It's how I check in with friends, see what's up, and get out of my own head for a minute. As an author, and a human, I have to remind myself that what happens in the "hallway" needs to stay there. I can't bring it with me into my work. In the times that I do, I go back to my written reminders. My journey. My path. My words. That's all I can control.

Maybe I make it sound easy but it's not. I get in these thought loops that make it hard to move forward. In my head, it sounds something like: *I don't belong here. Everyone is doing it better than me. I can't do this. I'm not making an impact.*

Being asked to be part of this anthology is a true full-circle moment for me.

It was Jennifer Probst's *Write Naked* that pulled me out of one such thought loop. I'd gotten so caught up in the hallway noise, I couldn't focus. Being reflective is important as a writer (and a human). Being overly critical is a hazard. Do yourself another favor and write down or save positive comments from readers about your words. Read those when you're feeling unsure. Remind yourself what *Write Naked* reminded me of: We are not alone. Everyone worries that the words they send out into the world will not be received in the way we intended. Knowing that even the authors I look up to and admire— the ones I'm influenced by—understand these feelings, have felt them, and worked through them (or continue to do so), made it easier to walk that analogical hallway with my head up more often.

Writing and publishing are hard. That's okay. Hard is not a synonym for impossible. I have days I feel like I've done all the things I planned to do and others where I wonder if I should just shut down the computer. Something I try to remember is that I write because it brings me joy. There are stories inside of me and I can only handle them wandering around my brain for so long. Some of those stories will be someone's favorite. They'll also be someone's least favorite. But they're mine, good or bad, and writing them down and then sharing them quiets the noise inside of my own head.

My power, and yours, as a writer, is offering the world a story that is uniquely and beautifully authentic. Someone else writing a story with similar themes or tropes does not negate the impact—quiet or loud—of our words.

Masters like Cezanne, Gaugin, and Van Gogh all created still-life art. Each of them contributed uniquely to that period, and while they may be compared and contrasted for discussion's sake, there is and was room for each of them to give us something visually different. Something only they could give. If given the same subject, they each would have painted from their own perspective.

It is the same for writing. Look up to other writers, be inspired and motivated by peers. Push yourself to do better, explore your own boundaries, but when you feel that white noise in your brain or start slipping down that rabbit hole, write. Pull yourself out the loop with words and remind yourself that what you have to say, matters. Your words matter. You matter.

Sophie Sullivan is a Canadian author as well as a cookie-eating, Diet Pepsi-drinking, Disney enthusiast who loves reading and writing romance in almost equal measure. She writes around her day job as a teacher and spends her spare time with her sweet family watching reruns of *Friends*. *Ten Rules for Faking It* is her romcom debut novel, but she's had plenty of practice writing happily ever after as her alter ego, Jody Holford.

Website: www.sophiesullivanauthor.com/
www.jodyholfordauthor.com/

Instagram: www.instagram.com/jody_
holford/
www.instagram.com/authorsophiesullivan/

THREE THINGS THAT CHANGED MY LIFE AS AN AUTHOR

Jen Snow

MY WRITING JOURNEY started at age five once I learned how to spell. At 15, I started collecting rejection letters after I submitted my first hand-written, young adult novel to Harlequin. So I've been on this rollercoaster ride for a long time. Have I loved every minute of it? Yes. Is it hard, unpredictable, and soul crushing at times? Also, yes.

But along the way, over the span of my professional career, three things changed my author life.

Block out the noise.

The first thing was deciding not to let other people's opinions, negativity, pessimism, or fear hold me back from going after my dream. When you're surrounded by people who don't share the same passion, it's difficult for them to understand the persistent desire to create that writers simply can't ignore. It's easy to listen to the advice of those who are too afraid to take risks and it's easy to believe all the negativity that comes from a place of fear of failure, fear of trying. But when I decided to block out the noise—even the well-meaning noise—my career took a turn for the better. I knew this career wouldn't be easy, but once I set my mind on achieving certain milestones, they were easier to achieve when I stopped listening to the naysayers and just got on with it.

The Year of No.

The second thing that changed my author path was what I refer to as my "Year of No." In 2017, I had five novels releasing, but every new proposal I submitted to publishers (including my current editors) was rejected. I wrote synopsis after synopsis, partial after partial, and even a full book that were all met with the same answer—no.

I threatened to quit writing every day that year, but it's just not in me to give up. Especially not on something that quite literally consumes me.

So, I took a break for a few weeks and re-evaluated how I was approaching things and what I could do differently. Something needed to change.

Turned out, I needed to step outside my comfort zone again. Just because I'd published 20 novels didn't mean I could get comfortable. My new ideas were coming from a slightly stagnant and—if I'm being honest with myself—lazy place. I'd reached a level of success and therefore had lost a little of the drive and ambition to get to the next level. So, I decided to go as far outside my comfort zone as possible and write a new book in a completely different genre.

I wrote a thriller that year and after many revisions, it sold … and it remains my bestselling book to date. It didn't launch a wildly successful thriller career, but it did renew my spirit and passion for writing. It pushed me outside my comfort zone and taught me that I could write anything I wanted, so I needed to think bigger. If I hadn't had that Year of No, I may never have been uncomfortable enough in my career to take another risk, to aim higher. So, to every one of those rejection letters, I cherish you.

Try something new.

The third thing to change my author life was voicing that I wanted to try writing a screenplay. I'd written plays in my youth and had always secretly wanted to write movies, but I wasn't sure how and, well, the film industry is impossible to break into, right?

There were more than enough excuses preventing me from actually doing it, but what made the difference was casually saying it out loud to a "friend" and getting the scoff. The one that implies, "yeah right, good luck." I'm not someone who is motivated by proving others wrong. My motivation comes from proving myself right, but in that moment, I realized this was another opportunity to do that.

So, I started reading scripts. I bought books on screenwriting. I bought screenwriting software. Then I started by adapting some previously published novellas. They were older and my writing had definitely changed (hopefully for the better) over the years, but the stories themselves were still fun and marketable, so I thought why not try to give them new life? It worked. I finished my first screenplay in 2018, attended a film conference that year, and came home with a manager and a bidding war on that first script. It was made last year as a TV movie and I got to see my name in movie credits for the first time.

Since that one released, it has opened many doors in the industry and I'm enjoying diversifying my writing in different formats. But the best part was realizing that no dream is out of reach with the right focus and hard work.

My writing journey has been full of ups and downs, like every other author I know, but what changed my author life along the way was always just believing in myself more than I doubted, by taking new risks when the old ones weren't scary anymore and by listening to my own voice above all the others.

XO

Jennifer Snow is a *USA Today* bestselling author writing contemporary romance fiction for Grand Central Publishing, Entangled, and Harlequin. Her stories range in heat level from sweet to sexy and are set everywhere from big cities to small towns. Her books are light and humorous, but also full of heart, featuring families and communities readers love to visit over and over again. Originally from Newfoundland, Canada, she now resides in Spain with her husband, son, and three mischievous cats.

She currently publishes psychological thrillers under her pen name J.M. Winchester and writes screenplays and TV shows in her "spare" time. Her holiday rom-com, *Mistletoe and Molly*, aired Christmas 2021!

Website: https://jennifersnowauthor.com/

Instagram: www.instagram.com/
jensnowauthor/

WHAT HAS HELPED ME MOST ON MY JOURNEY

Laura Pavlov

MY JOURNEY HAS been an exciting one thus far. I left teaching after 17 years to pursue writing full-time and it has been amazing and scary and overwhelming and inspiring, all at the same time. Is that a thing?

It's honestly the truth. When I first started this adventure two-and-a-half years ago, I didn't know what a beta reader was, or what an advanced reader copy was, or what cover reveals were. I didn't have an editor or a cover designer, I had very little experience with social media, and I had no idea what all was involved in this new career path that I was on.

I had this vision that I would be writing all day, every day, and while I do write a lot … there is so much more involved in this journey. Being a self-published author means that you are both the author and the publisher. There are a lot of moving parts, and you will wear many different hats. But it's also fabulous and rewarding at the same time.

It's so important to be open to learning from everyone around you. Read everything you can about craft and marketing and social media. It's easy to get overwhelmed, and you won't have it all figured out with your first book, and that is *totally okay*. I hope that my writing gets better with each book, and my knowledge for publishing grows with each release as well.

I think it's most important to remember to write every day. It's easy to get distracted by all the things that need to get done, but I always set a certain amount of time aside just to *write*. At the end of the day, you can't put out a good book if you aren't getting those words in. So, make that your priority.

Don't be afraid to ask for help. I've met so many lovely people along this journey, some whom I now consider my closest friends. Ask questions. Listen to what other people are doing and what works for them—and then try *everything*. You have to find your own path, one that works best for you, but asking for help along the way is only going to make you better.

The most valuable advice that I could give would be to surround yourself with good people. Find an editor and team (developmental editor, copy editor, and proofreader) that you mesh well with and that will get you off and running. Editing is so important. Get as many eyes on that manuscript before you send it out into the world. It truly does take a village, as your cover designer and promo team are also key. Surrounding yourself with people who encourage and support you is so important. I have two author friends who I write with every day, and we push one another, as well as hold one another accountable. It helps so much.

I would also strongly encourage you to get your newsletter and your Facebook reader group going. Building those relationships has been so beneficial for me. Those are your people. They are the ones who will download your book on release day and help spread the word by shouting it from the rooftops. I am so grateful for this supportive community. Share and thank the people who are cheering you on. I send out a lot of paperbacks as thank-you gifts, and bloggers and bookstagrammers really appreciate it.

Sign up for as many author classes and seminars writing, releasing, and running ads as you can. The more you expose yourself to, the more success you will have. Hear what others are doing. Find out what's working and what's not. Educate yourself on all the things, from running ads to how to promote your next release, by listening and learning from others in the book community. Cross-promote as much as you can; it's such a valuable way to meet author friends and find new readers at the same time. Share other authors' releases and be a cheerleader for those around you. Be kind and grateful for those who support you and do the same for them. There are so many books to choose from, and it's amazing when people want to read your work. Celebrate that.

Lastly, enjoy the ride. Set goals, but be sure to stop for a moment when you achieve them and celebrate those moments—big and small. It's easy to chase the next rung, but it's so important to be present and enjoy the ride. Remember, there is no right or wrong way to do this author gig. Find what works for you and then harness it. How lucky are we that we get to wake up every day and do what we love?

Laura Pavlov writes sweet and sexy contemporary romance that will make you both laugh and cry. She is happily married to her college sweetheart, mom to two awesome almost-grown kids, and dog-whisperer to one temperamental Yorkie and one wild Bernedoodle. Laura resides in Las Vegas where she is living her own happily-ever-after. Be sure to sign up for updates on new releases. Laura loves to hear from readers!

Website: www.laurapavlov.com

Instagram: www.instagram.com/laurapavlovauthor/

Facebook: www.facebook.com/LauraPavlovAuthor/

Tiktok: www.tiktok.com/@laurapavlovauthor

Read:

Always Mine

https://geni.us/AlwaysMineLP

**He fights fires for a living, but the flames
building between us may
be too big to extinguish.**

Niko West is the most beautiful man I've ever laid eyes on. Six feet, four inches of broody, chiseled Greek god in a firefighter suit. He's also been my best friend since kindergarten. He always says the only solid thing in his life is our friendship. He's Honey Mountain's favorite player and I'm what you'd call a relationship girl. But when I find myself single for the first time since turning sixteen, I make Niko an offer he can't refuse. *Who better to show me what I've been missing?* But now that we've crossed that line, I don't know if friendship is enough for me.

MARKET OR DIE

Willow Winters

MY MOTTO SINCE the beginning of this career has been the same. It's kept me going through the high highs and the low lows. Whenever I'm asked for advice, it's what I tell new authors who plan to self-publish. It occasionally gets pushback though. My motto:

Write for yourself.
Edit for the masses.
Market for the money.

If you guessed that it's that last line that sometimes receives hesitation, you'd be right. "Market for the money" throws so many people off—readers and writers alike. As if making decisions for income is an inherent negative. However, if you do not market for the money, how do you expect to be able to write at all? Self-publishing means you aren't just an artist, you're also a business owner. If your business side doesn't take care of your artist side, you will wither away. Creativity means nothing if you cannot fuel it. When we're talking about our work and our livelihood, that includes money.

So let's talk about how to earn more money with business decisions to make the most of the writing.

First off, market your work to as many readers as possible. There are so many avenues that can fall under "marketing." From the wording used to the covers and visuals readers see. When I think of marketing, my first thought is the cover. They say "don't judge a book by its cover," but it's a saying for a reason. We do judge books by their covers and so many potential readers are lost because a cover isn't what the reader is looking for or it's easily overlooked. Some readers want objects, some want discreet, others want a sexy cover ... there are so many different markets for the same exact story. So what's the solution? Put the same book in as many covers as you can.

My main branding includes romantic couples for the most part, but I also have a discreet series line, which includes all of my books in simple and plain covers. For my cliffhanger series, I always bundle them up, set a higher price and launch that with an "object" cover. For reference, check out my Merciless series versus its collection title, *All He'll Ever Be*. Two very different brandings and markets, yet it's the same story. Is it a lot of work? Yes. But I want a lot of readers, so it's worth it.

Secondly, funnel those readers and do everything you can to hold on to them. This means ensuring your backmatter gives every reader a call-to-action that will resonate with them. Call-to-actions can include:

- Preorder the next book.
- Sign up to my newsletter for an exclusive deleted scene. Join my Patreon for an extended epilogue.
- Follow me on social media so you can stay in the know with my new releases and sales and freebies.

You can offer readers so many different call-to-actions. Don't forget to include your other published books, too! Give them options for what they enjoy doing and what they want to do. Every reader is different and each one may be most comfortable only on a specific platform. So make it available to them and easy to find.

Thirdly, create as many revenue streams as possible. For one story we already know it could be cloaked in many different covers. But it can also be a graphic novel. It can be an audio book. It can be an incentive to join an author's Patreon. It can be the star of a Kickstarter featuring 3D gold foil sprayed edges special editions for collectors. That's just one book, with many different options for many different readers. The more options you create, the more readers you will reach. And the more income you'll receive off of a single book.

If I could give one last piece of advice: Always remember your passion and connect with readers genuinely. This will fuel your writer's side. Every day, I wake up to readers on so many different platforms reaching out for more, or with questions, or to simply tell me they loved my book. That will always motivate me to keep going.

Willow Winters started writing after having her little girl, Evie, December of 2015. She's noted many times that during her pregnancy with her she relied on books. She binge read romances, sometimes more than a book a day.

After her daughter was born, with stories in her head, and a sleeping baby on her chest who refused to be put down, Willow escaped into books again, this time writing them. The stay-at-home mom, turned prolific romance writer attributes much of her success to the romance reader community. "I never thought I would reach this point of success to be honest. It's insane to me that I have connected with so many readers and I love each and every one of them for all of their support. I'll be honest, some days are *hard*. I have my littles during the day and I write at night. Some days are just simply exhausting and then I hear from a reader and it motivates me to push through and keep writing. I couldn't be more grateful for this wonderful career."

Website: www.willowwinterswrites.com/

Instagram: www.instagram.com/
willowwintersshouldbewriting/

TikTok: www.tiktok.com/@
willowwintersauthor

Facebook: www.facebook.com/
AuthorWillowWinters

WHAT TO EXPECT WHEN YOU'RE ~~EXPECTING~~ WRITING

Ann Marie Walker

A S I SAT down to gather my thoughts on writing a novel, the book *What to Expect When You're Expecting* kept popping into my head, and why not? There's a lot of similarities between giving birth to a book and a baby. They take roughly the same amount of time and they both result in weight gain (hello stress eating while on deadline!) and sleepless nights. Although I have to admit, the nine books I've published were a lot easier on my boobs and varicose veins than the four kids!

But where to begin? For me, in the end, it was simple: Write what you love to read. If only it hadn't taken me three years to figure that out. Like so many at the time, I found myself inspired by Stephanie Meyers' success, which is why my first attempt at publishing came in the form of a young adult manuscript. I was determined, I will give myself that. I was not, however, a huge fan of young adult novels and I was definitely not cut out to write with a teen voice, something that took me approximately 75 rejection letters to accept! Eventually, I switched to the genre I love to read (romance) and went from 75 agent rejections to three offers of representation *in one week*. I'd like to say it was smooth sailing from there, but if you're reading an essay on the writing craft, you probably already know that nothing in this industry is that simple. After my "instant success," it took seven more years and contracts with three different publishing houses—resulting in four "digital-only" and three "print-on-demand" novels—before I finally walked into a bookstore and saw my "baby" on the shelf of a bookstore. And yes, I cried.

Then what? You've got an idea for a novel—one that could easily sit on the shelves right next to your all-time favorites—and you've even found the perfect table at Starbucks at which to write your masterpiece. But how do you go from middle-of-the-night inspiration to middle-of-the-day word count? When people ask about my writing process, I tell them it's almost always the same. I start with the "meet cute" (or "not so cute" in the case of my enemies-to-lovers books) and from there I figure out what will pull them apart (their dark moment) and what will bring them back together for their "happily ever after." Sometimes I know their names from the start, others require days on baby naming sites (which brings on a myriad of baby gadget ad placements, something that, come to think of it, likely contributes to the analogy I made at the beginning of this essay) until I find one that fits the personality of a person I'm slowly piecing together in my head. After that, I conjure the setting, which can—as in the case of my small-town romance off the coast of the Carolinas or my transatlantic rom-com set in both Dublin and Malibu—almost become a secondary character.

Speaking of the supporting cast, don't worry if you don't have one. At least not right away. Friends and family, or enemies and adversaries for that matter, will present themselves along the way. My first draft isn't really a draft at all, but rather a general outline. I know the broad strokes, but a side character—even one who turns out to be so popular people ask if they can have their own book—often won't exist at all in the first one hundred pages. Which brings me to the part where I will sound like the little kid from that M. Night Shyamalan movie. You know, the one who whispered, "I see dead people." Only for me, and many other authors I've spoken to, it's more like, "I hear fictional people." It might sound a bit crazy, but once I get going with a novel, the scenes tend to play in my head like a movie. Something readers tell me quite frequently is that they could "see" the book as they read (or in one case, even hear the character's accent). I can't think of a higher compliment, one I totally attribute to the time I spend not typing per se, but rather imagining every detail as though I'm actually watching the scene instead of merely writing it.

In this industry, most authors categorize themselves as either plotters or "pantsers," those who fly by the seat of their pants. I guess I'm both. So my advice comes down to this: Know your starting point and destination, but be open to detours along the way. And when you get stuck, go for a walk, watch a movie, or just let yourself daydream. You never know where you might end up.

Ann Marie Walker is the author of nine novels, ranging from romantic suspense to romantic comedy. She's a fan of fancy cocktails, anything chocolate, and '80s rom-coms. Her superpower is connecting any situation to an episode of *Friends*, and she thinks all coffee cups should be the size of a bowl. You can find her at AnnMarieWalker.com, where she would be happy to talk to you about alpha males, lemon drop martinis, or Chewbacca, the Morkie who is kind enough to let her sit on his couch. Ann Marie attended the University of Notre Dame and currently lives in Chicago.

Website: www.annmariewalker.com/

Instagram: www.instagram.com/annmarie_ walker/

Facebook: www.facebook.com/ AuthorAnnMarieWalker/

Twitter: https://twitter.com/annmarie_walker

WRITE BETTER FASTER

Pippa Grant

I WAS SIXTEEN YEARS into my writing journey when I found the one thing I wish I'd had from the start, and that's Becca Syme.

Becca's Better Faster Academy offers courses in getting to know yourself. Sounds like a weird thing to help with writing, right? But it's made all the difference not just in my professional life, but also my personal life.

The Better Faster Academy courses aren't about "you should always plot" or "character sheets are the only answer to well-developed characters." Instead, it's about "How am I built, and based on who I am, how do I work best?" Some authors plot. Some don't. Some write every day. Some don't. Some can tell you their characters' favorite color. Some can't.

And that's all absolutely okay.

Books get written—*good* books get written—no matter the process.

The fact that there are so many ways to write a book is why I'm such a believer in the Better Faster Academy. (This is not a paid endorsement—it's just changed my writing life that much.) Once I learned (and embraced) that I am *not* a plotter and that, based on my own personality, I should embrace not plotting, I let go of the stress of feeling like I *should* be a plotter, no matter which other successful authors around me swore by it.

Someone else's method will not write your books. I mean, it might. But will it write your books the best way for you? Learning what your own method is, and embracing how you work, and giving yourself the tools you need to work best, is not only a great way to streamline and hone your own methods, but for me, it's led to greater satisfaction in my work.

Greater satisfaction in my work leads to greater work.

Greater work leads to more personal satisfaction too, and the happier I am, the better I write.

It's this big, beautiful loop that I live in every day after learning (and re-learning, and re-learning) to let go of the expectations that come with taking other classes that tell me "The Secret to Writing Faster" or "The One Surefire Way to the Top of the Charts."

It has come with learning who I am and how I can be the best me; for me, that came from the Better Faster Academy.

If you're not a class person, the theory can still work. Embrace who you are. Embrace what works for you. Try new things, but be willing to let go of them if they don't help.

For me, the secret to success was finding the intersection between what the market wanted and what I wanted to write. I wanted to write funny books, but I needed to embrace tropes to succeed as a rom-com author. So I made the tropes as funny and outrageous as I could, letting go of all expectations and the limitations I'd put on myself to embrace what I truly loved, over and over again.

I followed my own path, reaching for my goals—in this case, hitting the top 100 on Amazon—not only doing it my way, but loving doing it my way, all the way to the top of the charts.

There's no easy secret to success, however you define it.

But being you—being *fearlessly* you—with or without the help of classes and coaches, is a fantastic step in the right direction.

Pippa Grant is a *USA Today* and #1 Amazon bestselling author who writes romantic comedies that will make tears run down your leg. When she's not reading, writing, or sleeping, she's being crowned employee of the month as a stay-at-home mom and housewife trying to prepare her adorable demon spawn to be productive members of society, all the while fantasizing about long walks on the beach with hot chocolate chip cookies.

Website: https://pippagrant.com/

Instagram: www.instagram.com/pippa.grant/

Facebook: www.facebook.com/
PippaGrantRomance/

Twitter: https://twitter.com/ReadPippa

THREE THINGS THAT CHANGED MY LIFE AS AN AUTHOR

Lena Hendrix

WHEN I FIRST started my writing journey, I was a thirty-seven year old mother of three, working full time. I had a burning desire in my bones to do *something* different. I was successful in my career and worked hard to be skilled in my area, but for a long time, it no longer felt like it was what I was meant to be doing.

It was something I was good at, but never a *dream job.*

Reading had always been a big part of my life and I couldn't help but daydream of a life filled with books and stories. When I finally decided that I would try independent publishing, I felt free. I love the entire process—from planning to being a discovery writer to learning from craft books. In the time I have been writing, I have learned so much from a variety of sources.

The top three things that changed my life as an author have been: mindset, continual learning, and treating my writing as a business from the beginning.

First, I decided to enter the world of publishing with a positive mindset. Sure, it would be great to have my debut novel be the breakout, but I also knew that was unlikely. However, if I chose to look at my writing as a long-lasting career and not a flash in the pan, I could focus on the things that would positively impact my career over time:

Write the next book.

Make goals that are not tied to finances but still move the needle forward.

Cheer on other indie authors and support them whenever I can.

Find the lesson in the good and bad things that happen.

Another of the most significant impacts on my writing career has been to be open to learning as much about the craft of writing as I can. I continue to learn every day. I listen to podcasts, attend virtual conferences, and consume a ridiculous number of craft books.

When I read through craft books, I almost always get the paperback version (versus an e-book) because I flag sections, write notes in the margins, and highlight things that stand out. This helps because when I feel stuck, I can go back through the books and flip to a section and reread what stood out to me. I almost always leave with another morsel of information that I can apply to my work-in-progress.

Also, if a more established author who I respect

speaks, I listen. There are a lot of authors who have been publishing a lot longer than I have and if I listen carefully enough, willingly impart invaluable information. Sometimes, what they were saying wasn't what I wanted to hear, but more often than not, they were correct. The indie writing community is full of extremely generous souls who will share everything you need to know to set yourself up for success.

Speaking of setting up for success, the final thing that I believe helped me launch a successful career was treating my writing as a business from the beginning. When I set out writing, I was working full-time and writing in stolen moments around work and bedtimes and my kids' after school activities.

However, that didn't stop me from treating my author business *as a business*. Some of the ways I did this was to set up an LLC and a separate business bank account. This way, it was very clear that my writing was a business and it was easy to keep all of those finances separate from the beginning.

Also, I was sure to hire a professional cover designer and an editor right away. If I wanted a place at the table with the more established authors, I knew that I had to produce a product that was going to be on par with what my readers expected. I pulled cover images of comparable authors to see what was working—couples versus a man, warm versus cool, bold versus soft. I made decisions that were in the best interest of the business, regardless of my personal preferences. A proper cover also helped me convey the subgenre and heat level of my romances. With the proper cover to entice readers to try my book, I then had an editor polish my writing to keep readers engaged and coming back for more.

All in all, there's likely a million tiny things that have changed my career as an author, but the most impactful have been maintaining a positive mindset, learning as much as I can about the craft of writing, and making key decisions based on a business mindset and not only personal preferences. Writing has gone from something I dreamed of doing to a career that brings me more joy that I could have anticipated.

For any aspiring authors reading this, go for it! Chase that dream and hold on to it. It's worth it.

Lena Hendrix is a contemporary romance author living in the Midwest. Her love for romance stared with sneaking, racy Harlequin paperbacks and now she writes her own hot-as-sin small-town romance novels. Lena has a soft spot for strong alphas with marshmallow insides, heroines who clap back, and sizzling tension. Her novels pack in small town heart with a whole lotta heat.

When she's not writing or devouring new novels, you can find her hiking, camping, fishing, and sipping a spicy margarita!

Amazon: www.amazon.com/Lena-
Hendrix/e/B091W1QLQC

Tiktok: https://vm.tiktok.com/ZMe93ExoP/

IG: www.instagram.com/authorlenahendrix/

FB: www.facebook.com/lenahendrixwrites

Read:
Finding You
https://geni.us/findingyou

Lincoln Scott is a retired Marine searching for the woman whose letters saved his life. When Joanna James finds her way back to his small town, he quickly realizes she's the "Jo" he's spent years searching for. One problem—she's his brother's best friend and his new summer employee. Lincoln is faced with an impossible choice—his honor or his heart.

WRITING SUCCESS: IT'S MATHEMATICS, NOT MAGIC

Dylan Newton

TO SET THE record straight: I hate math. I was an English major in college, and while my first career was in banking, it was always words—not numbers—that drove me. Yet, when I'm asked by writers for tips to become traditionally published, they're often disappointed that my tricks for writing success aren't magical. They're mathematical. Yuck, right? Yet, read on, my writing friend, because while the path to publishing is dry and prosaic, if you apply the formula below, you will achieve your writing goal.

Add up the words until your book is finished.

It sounds simple, but finishing your book is the hardest part of becoming published. Create a weekly wordcount goal or time for your butt in the chair to write—whichever works best for you and your schedule—then commit to this number. I don't believe in writer-shaming, so to those who decree that "real" writers *must* write every single day, I say: Nonsense. I don't write every single day, neither do most published authors I know with jobs, kids, spouses, and life responsibilities. But it is necessary to set a weekly writing number of words or time—things that can be measured and calculated. This mathematical goal can be small, and should be realistic. Plan out your minimum word count or writing time every week, and force yourself to sit there until you're finished. It's grueling. Sometimes it sucks so bad I'd rather clean than sit at the computer for one more minute. You'll have those moments, too. But you'll also have days when you're in the groove, your sentences flowing into tidy paragraphs, building up chapters like a tower of Legos. That feeling—the writer's high—keeps me in my seat, plunking at those keys. Need a jumpstart? Consider joining National Novel Writing Month challenges (www.nanorwrimo. org) to establish the mathematical habit of writing a certain word count per day—I'm a fan, and lean on this fantastic partnership of writers to hit word counts.

You are ready to be a writer. Today.

Write what you love, with your unique voice and perspective. You don't need an M.F.A. or a B.A. or any of that B.S. If you can string a sentence together, you are ready to be a writer. Will you improve the more you write? Absolutely. But that does *not* mean you wait until you're perfect before you start ... because perfection is as obtainable as memorizing all the numbers of Pi. Writers improve and evolve constantly. Beware of perfection that disguises itself as research—a common procrastination technique. Force yourself to write past what you don't know, and use my tip for places where you need to research: Put an XX to stand in for those words. I use this technique to stave off the proverbial writer's block. The days I'm stuck in a scene, I set a timer and spend a half-hour researching one XX placeholder. When the timer goes off, I write what I discovered, and this usually results in completing that scene. This XX trick keeps those words flowing and ensures your ignorance doesn't stop your creative freight train from chugging down the track. Math is methodical, and if you use the above trick, so is writing.

Add to your writer's toolbox and increase your writer friends.

Reading books on writing and having a writing accountability group keeps me sharp and encouraged in this lonely occupation. Both help me hit word count goals, which keeps my writing on a mathematical trajectory to success. My writing friends help proofread, brainstorm, or are there to give support (and chocolate) when I'm filled with self-doubt. Don't have writing craft books or writer friends? Chances are, your local library does. Libraries are a writer's best friend, so be sure to visit yours for writing resources, groups, or even a protected place to write, safe from the distractions of home. Not much of a social butterfly? Join an online writing community, instead. Magic happens when you add writers together, as more minds looking at your plot problem equals a solution.

Revise and subtract the unnecessary from your completed book.

New writers often think the first complete draft is the final draft, and they're unpleasantly surprised to discover they're wrong. Here's a writing fact: Good books aren't made in one draft, and writers are often blind to their book's problems. Before you submit, find readers or writing friends to review your draft and spotlight the book's plot holes, character inconsistencies, and general areas for content and line edit revisions. This is delicate work, so find people who can provide constructive, not destructive, feedback for improving your book. Avail yourself of self-editing tools to ensure your finished product is the tightest version of itself you can create *within a time limit.* Don't commit to perfection, but do commit to editing with a deadline for submission or publication.

Adding up multiple "Nos" can yield a single "Yes."

When you finally submit your novel to agents or publishers, you should prepare to hear "No" more often than "Yes." Think of your "No" answers as a badge of honor, as every published author has faced the "No"-foe, and gone on to succeed. I had a binder, fat with rejections, until becoming traditionally published. Even after that, while my books were available online, I wanted a publisher who could place them on bookshelves everywhere, so I set out to find an agent. I collected more "No" answers, learning along the way. Finally, I got my agent and I wrote more books when others didn't sell, determined to see a novel of mine in every bookstore in America. I racked up some additional "No" answers until finally getting the "Yes" that made all the difference. "No" only equals "The End" if you stop writing.

There you have it: My five-step formula for writing with a goal to publish. At the heart of it, being a successful writer of words is less about magic ... and more about mathematical perseverance.

Dylan Newton was born and raised in a small town where the library was her favorite hangout.

After over a decade working in corporate America, Dylan quit to pursue her passion: writing books. When she isn't writing, Dylan is pursuing her own happily-ever-after with her high school sweetheart as they split time between Florida and Western New York with their two much cooler daughters.

Dylan's romantic comedy *How Sweet It Is* was starred by Kirkus Reviews and quoted as "a hilarious rom-com romp that delivers on both sweet and heat."

Read:
How Sweet It Is
Kindle Store

Check her out at www.DylanNewton.com

Facebook: www.facebook.com/
DylanNewtonAuthor

Instagram: www.instagram.com/
authordylannewton/

YOU MEAN I HAVE TO ... *WRITE?*

April Asher (April Hunt)

CONTRARY TO WHAT I say to my teenager (that mother knows *all*), I don't. (Shhh, don't tell them.) But one thing on which I'm 100 percent certain is: *You can't edit a blank page.*

We've all seen the inspirational phrase around Instagram and posted on writers' desktop marquees, and do you know why?

Because it's true.

As badly as writers would love to bypass the dreaded rough first draft for one that gleams so bright it requires heavily tinted sunglasses when in direct eye contact, that first pile of words needs to happen. It doesn't have to be perfect. Hell, it *won't* be perfect. I think that's why a lot of creatives (myself *definitely* included) fear that first draft. Because after all, we are our own worst critics.

My first drafts are *rough*. I'm talking gaping holes and rusty, serrated edges that would require medical intervention—and tetanus shots—if they were to break the skin. You'd more than likely find a character called Violet on one page and Rose on the next. You'd *definitely* find countless passive verbs, cliched phrases, and crutch words. So many first drafts that after combining them, you'd get a collection larger than the Anita Blake series.

I know this about myself, and even after publishing multiple books, I often find myself instigating extreme avoidance tactics—even closet organizing the deep, dank abyss that is called my kids' rooms—to avoid getting the words down because I know they won't be the *right* words.

To this day, I need to remind myself that it's okay for the draft to be rough around the edges. (I'm a nurse. If it cuts me, I'll give myself my own damn tetanus shot.) I have to tell myself repeatedly that it's fine if the first words popping into my head are the most snooze-worthy or grammatically incorrect jumble of the alphabet I've ever written.

The first draft is meant to be a gooey slab of clay that you throw on the spinning table. It's probably misshapen, dry in some places, and a little wet in others. And yeah, it might resemble the poop emoji more than it does a work of art, but do you know what happens after you've finished throwing that clay slab on the table?

It's time to mold it.

Using your creative mind, the second draft is when you beautify that clay with hills and valleys. You smooth out those choppy sentences and hunt for those passive verbs until your creative mind begins to see the gleaming possibilities beneath. Is it daunting? It can be. I'm not going to lie. I can't tell you how many times I sat at my computer and stared at a first draft, wondering how I'd be able to transform it into something someone could read, much less enjoy.

It's a doubt I experience with *every* book I write.

But do you know what I say to myself, and what I want every creative to keep in mind when that doubt kicks in?

You already did the hard part. Whether it resembled a rusty tetanus trap or a poop emoji, you threw down those words into that Word doc, or notebook, or into Scrivener. Filler words. Crutch words. Maybe *all* the words. Now it's time for the magic to happen.

It's time for *your* magic to happen.

You don't need to find the perfect words in the first draft. The words just need to *be*. You'll get there. One word at a time. And if you ever need someone to remind you, reach out to any fellow writer and I guaran-damn-tee you that they'll tell you the same thing.

You got this.

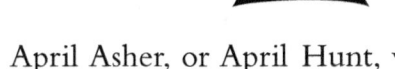

April Asher, or April Hunt, was hooked on romantic stories from the time she first snuck a bodice-ripper romance out from her mom's bedside table. She now lives out her own happily-ever-after with her college-sweetheart husband, their two children, and a cat who thinks she's more dog—and human—than feline. By day, April dons dark blue nursing scrubs and drinks way too much caffeine. By night, she still consumes too much caffeine, but she does it with a laptop in hand, and from her favorite side of the couch.

From the far left cushion, April Asher pens laugh-out-loud romantic comedies with a paranormal twist, but when she's not putting her characters into embarrassing situations with supernatural entities, she also writes high-octane romantic suspense as April Hunt, her thrill-seeking alter ego.

Website: www.aprilhuntbooks.com/

Instagram: www.instagram.com/novelsbyapril/

Facebook: www.facebook.com/
NovelsByApril

Twitter: https://twitter.com/NovelsByApril

THE NEED TO WRITE

A.L. Jackson

ONE OF THE hardest parts of writing is our tendency to compare ourselves to others. It's not a new topic or idea, but one I truly feel is incredibly important to address because it can be one that ends careers before they get started.

We have a tendency to look around at what everyone else is doing. We look at who we consider super successful authors, and when times get rough (or even before they do), we think we couldn't possibly achieve that status.

But I think sometimes even more dangerous is when we look at other writers who maybe started at the same time as we did and think our journey should be exactly the same.

We might feel that we've fallen behind. Or maybe that we write slower than others and we're not producing the same amount as everyone else. Perhaps our sales or ranking does not match up or even we have less of a social following.

It's those types of comparisons that often

lead us to question if we're cut out for writing at all. It's one thing I often hear in the author world—writers questioning if they really are a writer. That is one of the most discouraging places to be, and it can steal every ounce of inspiration that we have.

I think each one of us has felt that way before. We get to the lowest place where it seems hopeless—a useless endeavor that has us spinning our wheels or maybe has us curled up in bed in the fetal position.

My question I always pose is: *Do you feel like you have to write?* Is there a burning desire inside you demanding that you put the words on the page? Do you have characters that shout so loudly in your head that you can't quiet them?

To me, that is what makes a writer. It is someone who is compelled to share the stories inside them with others no matter the circumstances.

It feels like an intrinsic calling.

Listen to it.

That is the passion required to help get us through the difficult times. The moments when it feels impossible. When it seems we are never going to catch a break. When we get negative reviews, or we have a release that didn't meet our expectations.

And that leads us right back to the same place of looking around us at what everyone else is doing and questioning if we're cut out for it.

To me, for longevity, we have to be able to tap into that passion that absolutely drives us. The part of us that sings when we bring characters to life. The part that dreams of new worlds. Let that be the part that instills that determination within you.

And this doesn't mean that we don't look to others for inspiration, that we don't learn from those who we admire for help and guidance.

It means believe in your own, personal journey.

Grab a journal and revisit where you began. Go back to the very beginning. What drove you to put that first word on the page? What feeling did you possess? Do you still have it now? Take some time to remind yourself of it.

Let it feed the drive to overcome the hurdles that each of us face, and remember, you were meant to do this.

A.L. Jackson is the *New York Times* and *USA Today* bestselling author of contemporary romance. She writes emotional, sexy, heart-filled stories about boys who usually like to be a little bit bad.

Her bestselling series include The Regret Series, Closer to You, Bleeding Stars, Fight for Me, Confessions of the Heart, Falling Stars, and Redemption Hills. Watch out for her upcoming stand-alone, *Never Look Back*.

If she's not writing, you can find her hanging out by the pool with her family, sipping cocktails with her friends, or of course with her nose buried in a book.

Website: www.aljacksonauthor.com/

Instagram: www.instagram.com/
aljacksonauthor/

Facebook: www.facebook.com/
aljacksonauthor

TikTok: https://www.tiktok.com/@
aljacksonauthor

ADVICE FOR AN
ASPIRING AUTHOR

Joanna Rakoff

WHEN I WAS first starting out as a writer, I took a job at a literary agency, assisting a longtime agent who'd gotten her start—and made her name—doing what's known in publishing as "first serial," which basically means placing clients' short stories and essays and articles in magazines. And if that sounds like gibberish to you, "placing" means sending out writer's shorter work to magazine and newspaper editors. Some of the younger agents focused on signing new, interesting fiction and memoir writers, including some writers I loved at the time (and still love, like Mary Gaitskill and Melanie Thernstrom, both of whose work has had a huge influence on me).

At first, my job largely consisted of typing my boss' correspondence, dull letters asking for changes in book contracts and suchlike. As the months wore on, the younger agents realized I was underemployed and exceedingly bored, and they began giving me manuscripts to read, often from recent graduates of the most prestigious MFA programs—the Iowa Writers Workshop and Columbia University—but sometimes friends of current clients or friends of friends. Most of what I read was bad or dull or had potential, but definitely needed several more rewrites and perhaps the guiding hand of an editor. This didn't bother me at all, because no matter how bad the manuscript, it meant that I'd be called into an agent's office to discuss it, and I loved these conversations—often frantic, always fun—more than anything. The agents were so smart, and so passionate about their work; they truly loved literature, ushering great books into the world, and discovering new writers and building their careers. Each manuscript I read for an agent represented a potential new client, a potential new book, a potential new voice in the world.

Often, at writing conferences or when I speak to audiences, someone—or many people!—ask me what they need to do to get published. Do they need more followers on social media? Do they need a blog? A podcast? Should they be trying to write op-eds for the *Times*? Or a Modern Love piece? Do they need to write about trauma? Or about politics?

And every time I'm asked this question, I think back on those young agents, so hungry for great books to sell, so excited by writers with promise. I think back on that grand dame agent whom I assisted, sifting through stories, trying to find one that had a shot at landing in *The New Yorker* or *Harper's*. The world has changed a lot since I worked at the agency, certainly, but the vocation of the agent—and the editor—has not. All they want is a great story, a great essay, a great novel to publish. They don't care about your Twitter followers or your Instagram feed. They want great work. Truly great work.

The advice I always give at those conferences and the advice I'd give to any aspiring writer is that the one thing you need to do to get published is: Write a great book. That's it. Great work will find an agent, an editor, readers.

On a day-to-day level, what this means is even more simple: *Write.* Write the book you want to read. Write into the hole you see in the literary universe. Write the book you *know* the world needs. Write every day, if you can. But if you can't—because you have a demanding job or four kids or an aging parent who needs constant care—don't worry about it; write when you can. But make sure you're not letting life get in the way of writing. When my kids were tiny, I woke up at 5 a.m. to write, before the rest of the house jumped out of bed and began asking me for things; I wrote on my lunch break at work, rather than meeting friends or working straight through or planning meetings for that time; and I wrote after the kids went to bed, usually falling asleep with my head on my marked-up manuscript. I tell you this not to hold myself up as some example of superhuman writerly perfection, but simply to say: There are ways.

You will find them.

And though I began this essay talking about publishing, about agencies and agents, about the business of selling literature, the only path forward involves forgetting about those exact things. Don't try to game the system, to find the magic bullet that will shoot you onto the bestseller list, to figure out exactly what agents and editors and readers want. Instead, write, write, write, like your life depends on it, feel your way forward and don't stop until you've written the book—or story, or essay—that you want to read, that you need to read. If you do so, trust me, others will read it, too.

Joanna Rakoff is the author of the international bestselling memoir *My Salinger Year* and the novel *A Fortunate Age*, winner of the Goldberg Prize for Fiction, the Elle Readers' Prize, and a *San Francisco Chronicle* bestseller. Rakoff's books have been translated into twenty languages and nominated for major prizes in the Netherlands and France. She has written frequently for *The New York Times*, *Vogue*, *Marie Claire*, *O: The Oprah Magazine*, and many other publications.

The film adaptation of *My Salinger Year* stars Margaret Qualley as Joanna and Sigourney Weaver as her boss. Directed by Oscar-nominee Philippe Falardeau, the film opened in sixty-five countries in 2021, and is available for streaming wherever you rent movies.

Website: www.joannarakoff.com/
Instagram: www.instagram.com/joannarakoff

Twitter: https://twitter.com/joannarakoff

BOOK MARKETING FROM YOUR COUCH

Jennifer Bardsley

WHETHER YOU ARE on a budget or have an elite public relations firm working on your behalf, social media is a great way to connect with readers from the comfort of your couch. But building your author platform can also be draining, which is why it's important to have a plan. The first step is self-analysis. What are your skills? Are you better at witty one-liners, videos, or taking pictures? Next, you need to identify the demographics of your audience and where they are most likely to hang out online. The final step is the most difficult, high-quality content creation. Social media can be confusing, but it can also be an author's best friend.

When I signed my first book deal back in 2015, my agent told me to start a Twitter account. I followed her advice and did so, slowly building my follower count. But what I really loved was Facebook. That platform came naturally to me. Facebook felt like my living room. Twitter was the Wild West. Some authors thrive on Twitter, but it made me nervous. I kept my Twitter account, but I also opened a Facebook page I called "The YA Gal." By the time my first book was published in 2016, I had a large following there. Later, when I shifted into writing sweet romance, I changed the name of my Facebook page to "Jennifer Bardsley Author." Now, it not only helps me connect with readers, but Facebook has paid me bonus money because my traffic is so high.

Understanding who your readers are and where they spend their time online is critical. Are they old or young? Do they spend their time on computers or phones? On social media, demographics matter. Younger readers are more likely to be on TikTok or YouTube. Older readers are more likely to be on Facebook or Instagram. Yes, there are exceptions, but if you're writing cozy mysteries about a seventy-two-year-old lady detective, marketing your book on TikTok is probably a bad idea. If you're writing middle-grade fiction geared to kids, you might want to focus on making cute videos to share on YouTube. For political or nonfiction writers, a strong Twitter presence could be important. Find the match between your skillset and where your audience is most likely to be.

"Buy my book! Buy my book! Buy my book!" Nobody wants to hear that. One of the biggest mistakes authors make on social media is sounding spam-y. A better strategy is to offer content that appeals to your audience and occasionally talk about your book. For example, I know that my readers like to discuss literature, movies, pop culture, and issues that impact women. I share content about these subjects 90 percent of the time. I build a relationship with readers over shared values. Then, when I do mention my book, it's a natural part of the conversation instead of sounding like an advertisement. To make things easier on Facebook, I schedule posts ahead of time using Creator Studio in Facebook's professional dashboard. To simplify Instagram, I take dozens of pictures in one day and then use those pictures throughout the month. I think of it as meal prep. It's easier to cook dinner if you've already chopped the vegetables.

Book marketing from your couch shouldn't be a chore. The most important advice I can offer about social media is to have fun. Maybe there is a well-paid marketing team from a giant publishing house behind you, or perhaps this is your first book as an indie author. If you enjoy building your author platform, it will never be work. So pour yourself a cup of tea, put on a cozy pair of wool socks, and snuggle up on the sofa. You can reach readers all over the world from the comfort of your home.

Jennifer Bardsley is the author of *Sweet Bliss*, *Good Catch*, *The History of Us*, and more. A graduate of Stanford University, she lives in Edmonds, WA with her husband and two children. Jennifer's "I Brake for Moms" column has appeared in *The Everett Herald* every week since 2012. She also writes Young Adult Paranormal Romance under the pen name Louise Cypress. When she's not writing books, you can find Jennifer walking from her house to the beach every chance she gets.

FB: www.facebook.com/
JenniferBardsleyAuthor/

IG: www.instagram.com/
jenniferbardsleyauthor/

Website: www.jenniferbardsley.com

Read:
Sweet Bliss:

When Toby spotted the harbor seal, Julia knew that meant trouble. Her chocolate Labrador was a lot of things—loyal, affectionate, devilishly handsome—but clever wasn't one of them. Over the past six months of their relationship, Julia had cursed his pedigree on more than one occasion. If there were just a smidgen of shelter mutt in him, maybe he'd be smarter. Now, her adorably clueless puppy was swimming into open waters, and all Julia could do was scream at the top of her lungs. "Toby, come back!" Julia cupped her hands around her mouth and shouted so loud her throat hurt.

Purchase link:
https://www.amazon.com/gp/product/
B08JLWSZHF/

A List for
Aspiring Writers

Susan Stoker

Don't let anyone tell you "how" to write; figure out what works for you on your own.

Some authors will say that you *have* to write every day, or you *have* to have a beta reader, or you *have* to use at least three proofreaders. But what they're really doing is telling you what *their* writing process looks like. You have to figure out what works for you.

Be consistent.

Don't skip around in writing genres; don't write a long series, then a standalone, then a trilogy. You want your readers to know what to expect from you without even having to read the blurb. You want them to be one-clickers, and not have to "decide" if they'll like your newest book.

Also, be consistent with how many books you publish per year. If that's one book, great, make it the best one book ever. If that's 10 books a year, good for you! But if you have one book, then five, then 11, then two, it confuses readers and they won't know when you're publishing ... and you could lose them.

Write what you love from the start. Maybe some authors start out writing what is "popular" or what they think will make them money, then find out they don't even *like* writing that genre. If you start out writing what you love, it'll make it easier to finish that book (and the next and the next and the next).

Get the words on paper. You can always go back and edit later, but you can't edit what isn't there. Don't be one of those people who says at family gatherings, "I've been writing my debut book for five years." Don't analyze what you're writing as you write it. Get lost in the story, finish it, *then* go back and edit.

Susan Stoker is a *New York Times*, *USA Today*, #1 Amazon, and #1 *Wall Street Journal* bestselling author with a heart as big as the state of Tennessee, where she lives, but this all-American girl has also spent the last eighteen years living in Missouri, California, Colorado, Indiana, and Texas. She's married to a retired Army man (and current firefighter/EMT) who now gets to follow her around the country.

She debuted her first series in 2014 and quickly followed that up with the SEAL of

Protection Series, which solidified her love of writing and creating stories readers can get lost in.

Website: www.stokeraces.com/

Facebook: www.facebook.com/
authorsusanstoker

Instagram: www.instagram.com/
authorsusanstoker/

**Start The Refuge series with
Deserving Alaska:**
www.stokeraces.com/deserving-alaska.html

THE THREE SECRETS OF SUCCESS

Kristen Ashley

THE WRITING GAME is a hectic business. It's about creativity. It's about hustle. And if you're independently published (or even if you're not), you're going to need to tap into both sides of your brain to be a success at it.

There's so much to say about this, as you know, considering you're reading this book. But along my journey, I've found the following are the three things that are most important to being a successful author—from that creative spark all the way through to readers reading your work.

These are in order of importance:

1. Be authentic.

I'm talking about this in your craft. I'm talking about it in how you run your business. Also marketing. Also reader care. In fact, everything.

But primarily, it's in craft.

You've heard the saying, "Dance like no one is watching."

Well, write like no one will be reading … but you.

Write what *you* love to read. Don't write what's popular (unless you love it) or what you think a publisher will want (unless you dig it) or what an agent might like (unless you're into it).

Write for you.

I wrote books no publisher or agent would touch *for years*, until I published them myself, and when readers loved them (and boy, did they love them), publishers wanted them.

If you free yourself, if you write *your* book, first, you'll enjoy the process all the more. Second, readers will feel it. Trust me. They are savvy, and they're along for your ride. So what kind of ride are you going to give them? One that hums with, "God, I hope a publisher likes this book." Or one that sings with, "God, *I was born to write this book!*"

Whenever I talk about this, I like to steal a great quote, "If you build it, they will come."

If you write what you love, believe in it, give authentically to the story, the characters, the process … readers will find it and they'll love reading it.

2. Be nurturing.

Outside writing books you love, your readers are the most important thing you've got.

Take care of them.

There are probably a thousand ways to do this, so many that another entire book could be written about them.

That said, not all these ways work for everyone. It's part about what you find comfortable, part what fits in your schedule (another book could be written about balancing your writing, your selling, and your actual life, but I won't get into that here), and the last part is what works. Don't be frightened to play. However, if it doesn't feel right to you, stop. If you love it, though it might not seem to hit, keep going for a while, readers might catch on. If it's taking all of your time, adjust or abandon (you need "you time" to write and live your life).

I used to answer or like every comment on my Facebook page. It actually hurt to stop doing that. To stop being so intimately involved (or as intimate as social media can get) with my readers. But I just simply no longer had the time. I asked myself the question: What do my folks want from me? Do they want me to like a Facebook post, or do they want me to write more books?

They answered that for me. Writing more books, of course!

Find the ways that work for you (go back to number one, but also be sure there are healthy doses of number three).

The benefits of this are incalculable. I've found readers are loyal and supportive, they'll stand by you, help you market by word of mouth, and they feel a part of your journey in positive ways that make the experience of writing a lot less lonely. Not to mention, they are, truly, the best of company, because you have a great starting point for your relationship: You have something you love in common.

Now, you might be thinking, "But I'm private." Or, "I'm a huge introvert."

I'll tell you, some of my most introverted author friends have *the best* presence on social media. They find their niche, their way to give and share, and it's awesome.

Your readers have spent money on you and time with you. Be careful to respect that ... and find ways you're comfortable in giving back.

3. Be professional.

In the end, this is a business. Yes, the product is one of creativity and imagination. But it's still a product that will be for sale.

Important: Don't think of that while you're creating it. Put that right out of your head. Write on with no restrictions, you authentic person!

But once it's done, understand that you have to flip to the other side of your brain and figure out how to sell it, and while you do that, conduct yourself like a professional.

Remember, *you* are your brand. So if you burn a bridge, you're burning the path back to you. If you're not respectful, others won't respect you.

Equally important, out there in the world—be it at a conference, in a zoom meeting, or on social media—you are an ambassador not only of your books and your brand, but of this business, and particularly your genre.

You can be authentic, you can be you, but remember whose name is on the book jacket. Even if it's a pen name, it always leads back to you.

In the end, the best way to become an author is just …

Write.

Kristen Ashley grew up in Indiana, has lived in Colorado and the West Country of England, but now she calls the Valley of the Sun home. Thus she has been blessed to have friends and family around the globe. Her posse is loopy (to say the least), but loopy is good when you want to write.

Kristen has published over 80 romance novels, her work has been translated into 15 different languages, she's sold more than five million books, and has won or been nominated for numerous awards. She's started the Rock Chick Nation as a way to give back to her readers. RCN has a variety of programs to promote a strong female community and has donated more than $180,000 to women's charities.

FB: Kristenashleybooks

IG: Kristenashleybooks

Twitter: KristenAshley68

Pinterest: Kristenashleybooks

Website: kristenashley.net

Read:
Making the Match,
www.kristenashley.net/titles/making-the-match/

THE POWER OF SELF-CARE

Lexi Blake

TAKE CARE OF yourself.

There are many aspects of this business that will try to knock you down. That can be said of any industry, but I'm talking particularly about publishing and the specific problems an author faces. It's an industry built on rejection. Every author who has tried to get their work published has faced it. Whether it comes from the gatekeepers in traditional publishing or the literary world's distaste for self-publishing, we all face criticism and rejection. This is a hard industry to handle if you're damaged and, as a class of people, writers tend to be super-duper damaged. The one thing I would tell you is to find a core of belief in yourself, in your work. You wrote the book for a reason. You wrote it because something deep inside you needed to tell this story in this way. Own it. Believe in your work and your voice as an author.

This is not to say you shouldn't allow helpful criticism to help you grow, but you have to learn the difference between an editor trying to teach you how to better word something and someone who can't stand the word *moist* so they gave you one star. I know that sounds weird, but it happens, and it's easy to take every single critical review to heart. Don't. The most important skill you can learn as you navigate this career is to accept that you cannot please all readers all the time. You can get ten five-star glowing reviews and a single one-star; guess which one you will remember? Do not allow that one bad review to steer the course of your career.

Be kind to yourself. If you have to read reviews, don't dwell on them. When you feel bad, pick your favorite book and go read those reviews. You'll be surprised. What you connected with sent someone else into a spiral that led to them wasting hours of their time writing a hundred-point analysis of why that book and author suck. You'll sit there and shake your head and wonder what that reader was smoking, but understand that bad reviews happen to good authors and to good books, and they are merely part of the job. When you're an author, you have to go in understanding that you will get job reviews every day and they will be public. So when it happens, cry a little, grab a glass of wine or cup of tea, and do what you should do—write more.

It gets easier. A hundred books later and I still come across a review that stings from time to time, but I don't take it to heart anymore because I learned something along the way.

My voice matters. So does yours. That book you are writing is a piece of your soul, and what you live through, what you learn, will come through in that book and it can help someone else. The story you're writing, the one you need to tell, is the same story that someone out there needs to read, that will connect that reader to your world. That story that one person hated will let someone else know that they are not alone.

So grab your armor, word warrior. You will face the slings and arrows of the outrageous fortune we call publishing, and it will be worth it. To you. To someone out there who needs to hear your voice. Take care of yourself because you matter.

Lexi Blake is a *New York Times* bestselling author who lives in North Texas with her husband and three kids. Since starting her publishing journey in 2010, she's sold over three million copies of her books. She began writing at a young age, concentrating on plays and journalism. It wasn't until she started writing romance that she found success. She likes to find humor in the strangest places and believes in happy endings.

Website: www.lexiblake.net/

Facebook: www.facebook.com/
authorlexiblake/

Instagram: www.instagram.com/
authorlexiblake/

Twitter: https://twitter.com/authorlexiblake

THREE THINGS THAT CHANGED MY LIFE AS AN AUTHOR

Monica Murphy

I'VE BEEN AT this authoring thing for a long time—I was first published under my original pen name, Karen Erickson, in 2006! I've seen a lot of trends, authors, publishers, etc., come and go. Like ... a lot. This career has been a roller coaster, let me tell you! Here are the three things that changed my life as an author. Take from it what you will.

Make friends and hold them close.

Don't do it for the clout or for what they can get you either. It's not about that. You need friends in this business that you can vent to, versus you venting, let's say, on social media. You need people who understand what you're going through, because they're going through it, too. Friends you can bounce ideas off of, gripe about industry stuff, celebrate the milestones, and get and give sympathy over the losses.

And it's okay if you lose some friends and gain others over time. Our lives change and shift. There are people I was close to ten years ago that I'm not as close to now, and that's okay. Just make sure you have good friends in your corner you can trust. It's so important. The friends I've had over the years have helped me so much, and I do my best to help them too. Friends keep us sane during the wild ride that is this career!

Take chances.

If there's something that you've been dying to write, do it. If a trend sparks an idea and you're consumed by the story, chances are readers will be, too. After reading a bunch of new adult books in late 2012, I took a chance in early 2013 and self-published my own new adult in early 2013. It completely transformed my career. *One Week Girlfriend* literally changed my life—all because I took a chance and wrote a book under a new pen name. If I'd been too scared or worried about publishing it, who knows what would've happened to me. Which brings me to …

Never give up.

Seriously. Don't give up. You have to hang on, even when it gets rough. When you have a bad book release. Or a bunch of bad reviews. Or a slow year. Maybe it's difficult to write because you're dealing with other things in your life. Maybe the ideas aren't coming either. All of the previous things have happened to me. Multiple times. Yet I don't give up. I keep plugging away. Did I mention the roller coaster ride this career is? It's so accurate. There are ups and downs. Highs and lows. Sometimes you're just coasting. Things aren't terrible, but they could be better. Then you're high again, and you feel on top of the world.

I have witnessed so many people who gave up. There are a handful of people who I met *way* back in the day at my first Romance Writers of America conference who are still writing. Like, less than a handful. There was a guest speaker at that conference who looked around the room and said, "There are about two thousand of you here, and most of you are going to give up. You're not going to make it." Ooh people gasped. They were shocked she would say such a thing, but she wasn't wrong. I remember thinking then, "I don't want to give up. I'm going to keep at it until I make it."

Have I "made it"? I'm not sure. I can make a living as an author, which is an absolute dream come true. Never giving up is the reason I still even have a career—it's that simple.

Monica Murphy is the *New York Times* and *USA Today* bestselling author of the One Week Girlfriend series, Billionaire Bachelors Club series, and The Rules series. Her books have been translated in almost a dozen languages and has sold over one million copies worldwide. She is both a traditionally published and an independently published author. She writes new adult, young adult, and contemporary romance. She is also *USA Today* bestselling romance author Karen Erickson.

She is a wife and a mother of three who lives with her family in central California on fourteen acres in the middle of nowhere, along with their one dog and too many cats. A self-confessed workaholic, when she's not writing, she's reading or hanging out with her husband and kids. She's a firm believer in happy endings, though she will admit to putting her characters through many angst-filled moments before they finally get that hard won HEA.

Website: www.monicamurphyauthor.com

Instagram: www.instagram.com/ monicamurphyauthor/

Facebook: www.facebook.com/ MonicaMurphyauthor

AUTHOR FRIENDS

Whitney Dineen

THERE ARE SO many things I could share about my authoring journey but, alas, I've been asked to pick the most important. Buckle up, because here it is—I wouldn't be nearly as successful as I am without my author friends.

Whether you are just starting out, have already published a few books and are looking for more success, or are just thinking about writing a book someday, author friendships are the best foundation you can build on.

Join groups. Follow writers you love and comment thoughtfully on their posts. (Let these relationships grow naturally, don't be pushy.) Join reader groups, author support groups, and think tanks—social media is full of these. Go to conventions and take classes, mingle. Plainly put, get yourself out there.

Here's what author friends can do for you that your other friends can't:

They will commiserate with you in a way that no one else can. They know the struggles you're dealing with and are learning ways to navigate the murky waters of authordom in a way you may not have thought of.

Many of my early readers (pre-publishing) are author friends. They catch glaring mistakes, plot holes, typos, etc., that you as the author probably aren't even aware of. After writing 80,000-plus words, you need fresh eyes.

Author friends can offer blurbs for your book. I don't know about you, but I always read a few of those before I click the buy button.

They are often willing to do newsletter swaps. Newsletter swaps are immensely helpful in finding new readers in your genre.

They can share their experience with advertising. If you're already published, you know what a thrill ride it can be finding the right keywords, targets, etc. With Amazon and Facebook forever changing their algorithms, authors are constantly required to up their advertising game. It's daunting to write the book, get an editor, find early readers, hire a cover designer, *and* promote and advertise. Long gone are the days when an author's only job was to be creative.

Author friends are hands-down the best cheerleaders! My first three books earned nominal success, but it wasn't until my fourth that I really hit my stride. I was on the cusp of giving up the writing gig after book three, but I decided to give it one last try. That fourth book was *Relatively Normal*. One author friend raked over it with a fine-tooth comb—going above and beyond the duties of an early reader.

Another said my cover was crap. She designed the cover it currently has, which has been a big part of the book's success, as readers really do judge a book by its cover. *Relatively Normal* hit number eight in the entire Amazon store. I couldn't have done it without my team, and I certainly didn't quit the game. I've gone on to author and co-author another 25 books.

I wrote my last completed series with an author friend. I had a fun idea for a book, but I didn't have time to write it on my own. I contacted Melanie Summers, pitched her the book, and asked if she was willing to give it a go. The first draft of *Text Me on Tuesday* was written within two weeks. We wrote five more books in that series, and have just started a new series.

Author friends have been the heart and soul of my eight-year-long authoring career. Writing can be isolating and lonely, so friends who know what it's like are invaluable.

The best advice I can give you is to go forth and make friends! And remember, friendship is a two-way street, so be prepared to give the same kind of support you're looking for.

******* I was invited to participate in this book by—wait for it—an author friend!*

Whitney Dineen is a *USA Today* bestselling author and rock star in her own head. While delusional about her singing abilities, there's been a plethora of validation that she's a fairly decent author (*amazing!!!*). After winning many writing awards and selling nearly a kabillion books (math may not be her forte, either), she's decided to let the voices in her head say whatever they want (sorry, Mom). She also won a fourth-place ribbon in a fifth-grade swim meet in backstroke. So, there's that.

Whitney loves to play with her kids (dazzle them with her amazing flossing abilities), bake stuff, eat stuff, and write books for people who "get" her. She thinks French fries are the perfect food and Mrs. Roper is her spirit animal.

Website: Whitney Dineen | Author for all women

Facebook: Whitney Dineen Author | Facebook

TikTok: authorwhitneydineen

Amazon author page: Amazon.com: Whitney Dineen: Books, Biography, Blog, Audiobooks, Kindle

THREE THINGS THAT CHANGED MY LIFE AS AN AUTHOR

Carly Phillips

I'VE BEEN IN this business since 1994 and I've been published since 1999. I've been with quite a few of the (formerly) Big Five New York publishing houses and Harlequin, but in 2013 I declined a contract and decided to take my career indie. This was, hands down, the best decision I have ever made. Having all the decisions in my hands has been career changing. I'm aware everyone operates differently. Personalities are not the same. Work ethic is not the same for all. For me, being in control has been key.

The most important things that I think an author needs are:

1. A quality product. Without books to sell, nothing else matters.

2. To know your market. Sometimes this goes

with stay in your lane—find the thing you love to write and study the market (covers, point-of-view, what's relevant, how things change) because once you do that, you can deliver.

3. To satisfy reader expectations. A reader will come back if they fall in love with your characters, plot, and content, and know that the next time they pick up your, for example, fantasy romance novel, they won't get a romantic suspense book. Sure, you can write all over the place, but expect it to be hard to find a loyal audience.

4. Consistent branding. Do your covers reflect what is inside the pages? More importantly, do they fit within the top sellers in your genre? If your cover stands out as different, that can be good. If it's way out there, readers will shy away from something that doesn't meet expectations. There's that word again. Reader expectations. Give the reader what they want and they will come back.

5. A publishing schedule. Whatever your productivity level, be consistent. Readers need to know when your next book is coming out so they can count on you.

The three things that changed my life as an author were:

1. Learning the craft. Without learning the ins-and-outs of writing, passive voice, goal, motivation, conflict, point of view choice, etc., I would not have a successful career. There

are many online places where you can learn, including craft books.

2. Paying attention. The Roman philosopher Seneca said: *Luck Is What Happens When Preparation Meets Opportunity* … and this is so true. I was watching morning television in 2001 when Kelly Ripa on *LIVE with Regis and Kelly* joked about starting a book club. I sent her a book … and became the first author with a romance on a nationally-televised book club (in the days before social media!). This book and opportunity put me on the map.

3. Leaving traditional publishing and taking my career indie. Career changing. Being in control of all things has been vital to continued success.

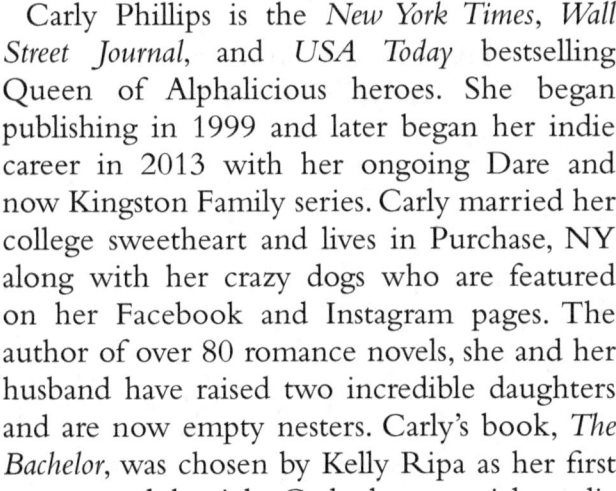

Carly Phillips is the *New York Times*, *Wall Street Journal*, and *USA Today* bestselling Queen of Alphalicious heroes. She began publishing in 1999 and later began her indie career in 2013 with her ongoing Dare and now Kingston Family series. Carly married her college sweetheart and lives in Purchase, NY along with her crazy dogs who are featured on her Facebook and Instagram pages. The author of over 80 romance novels, she and her husband have raised two incredible daughters and are now empty nesters. Carly's book, *The Bachelor*, was chosen by Kelly Ripa as her first romance club pick. Carly loves social media and interacting with her readers. Want to keep up with Carly? Sign up for her newsletter and receive *two free* books at *www.carlyphillips.com*.

Carly's Booklist: www.carlyphillips.com/

FB Group: Carly's Corner: www.carlyphillips. com/CarlysCorner

Facebook Fan Page: www.carlyphillips.com/ CPFanpage

Instagram:www.carlyphillips.com/ CPInstagram

Bookbub: www.carlyphillips.com/ CPBookbub

Amazon: www.carlyphillips.com/CPAmazon

Tiktok: www.tiktok.com/@ carlyphillipsauthor

THREE WAYS TO FIND YOUR AUTHENTIC VOICE

Jacquelyn Middleton

THERE ARE COUNTLESS "rules" about what we should and shouldn't do as authors, but here are three tips I found helpful in finding my authentic voice as an author.

1. Write for yourself.

When you spend so much time with your characters and settings, it's important to enjoy the process. There's nothing worse than slogging through a manuscript feeling like you're writing something you wouldn't actually read. That's why you should always write for yourself first. Creating a story you love is the best way to ensure that your work-in-progress will get finished.

So what does writing for yourself look like? First of all, it's choosing a point-of-view

(POV) you enjoy. I love all sorts of different POVs in books, but if I had to pick a favorite, I'd go with deep, third-person past, so that's the one I chose. I enjoy the flexibility, the deep descriptive dive into my characters, and the expressiveness of internal thoughts written in first-person present; plus it's just so much fun to write, and if it's fun to write, I'll keep hammering away until I type "The End." Find the POV that sparks your muse and write your heart out.

Writing for yourself also means writing about what interests you. Whether it be a love for royals or commoners, London or Los Angeles, hockey or knitting—writing about people, settings, or hobbies that own your heart will urge you to write further. Your enthusiasm will also translate on the page and captivate readers. Remember, if you're entertained, chances are your readers will be too.

2. Be yourself.

You know that Oscar Wilde saying about being yourself because everyone else is taken? That notion can apply to writing novels, too. As a reader, I love rom-coms. I can't get enough of them. However, when it comes to writing my own books, I know drafting a rom-com full of belly laughs isn't my jam and if I tried to write one, well, I wouldn't be true to who I am as an author. My strengths lie elsewhere. My books overflow with emotional messiness, are often angsty, and deal with topics some might call heavy, such as disenfranchised grief, panic attacks, Crohn's disease, and smiling depression (all of which I've either experienced personally or with loved ones). I want to share awareness, I want to bust stigma, and while my books do have funny moments sprinkled between the pages along with the swoony happy-for-now and happy-ever-after deliciousness, they should never be categorized as rom-coms. I always strive to be honest and upfront about what my books are (and aren't) with my potential audience because fibbing about the content and genre can backfire majorly.

We've all been there, right? You purchased a book based on its marketing, only to discover it's something completely different. Unfortunately, this type of hiccup happens often, and the fallout isn't pretty. Readers end up feeling deceived (rightfully so) and the author doesn't escape unscathed either. Often, they lose reader trust and end up being placed on a "never read you again" list. No one wins when the author or their books are marketed as something they are not.

Luckily, being yourself is one easy way to avoid this unwanted situation. Write what's in your heart and then celebrate (promote) the hell out of it, but always be honest about what it actually contains. When you're being your authentic self, you'll be gifting the world with a unique voice—yours—and no one else tells stories like you do.

3. Know yourself.

When you decide to write a novel, one of the biggest decisions you'll make is which publishing path to take: indie, hybrid, or traditional. There is no right or wrong decision. What matters most is choosing a path that works best for you. All three paths have different pros and cons.

I chose to take the indie route. Why? Well, I know myself all too well. I like—okay, let's be honest here—*need* the ultimate say in the creation of my books. As an indie, I decide my books' content, their covers, the interior design, my release dates, my books' titles, my choice of editor, and the extent of my marketing and publicity. You name it, I'll have a hand in it, and all these decisions reflect your brand as an author. As wonderful as traditional and hybrid publishing are, the authors don't always have much say in these areas, which would drop me into an epic anxiety spiral.

That said, with indie publishing there's a huge amount of work that goes beyond the actual writing of the book, and you're on the hook for a whole slew of financial aspects, too (editing fees, cover design fees, formatting, paperback proof printing, swag and prizes, shipping costs of review copies, marketing and promo fees, etc.). Paying for these things in advance and then hoping I earn back the costs is stressful. My anxiety doesn't always sit comfortably with this part of my indie author journey, but to me the benefits outweigh the negatives. I know I can handle these bumps in the road because the payoff, the freedom that comes with having a say in how and when I create, is so worth it, and when that first box of new books arrives and I can hold my hard work in my hands, it's the best feeling in the world. I wouldn't have it any other way.

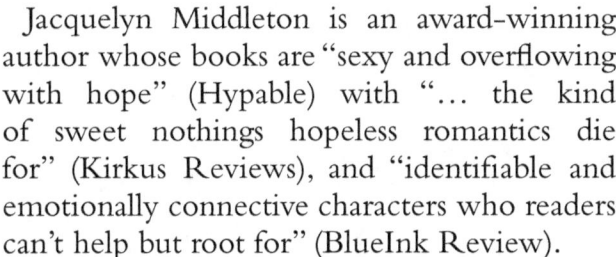

Jacquelyn Middleton is an award-winning author whose books are "sexy and overflowing with hope" (Hypable) with "… the kind of sweet nothings hopeless romantics die for" (Kirkus Reviews), and "identifiable and emotionally connective characters who readers can't help but root for" (BlueInk Review).

Jacquelyn writes love stories for hopeful romantics—"hopeful" because her novels are always optimistic and she believes "happily-ever-afters" are more important now than ever before. But life is messy, relationships are messy, and her books aren't afraid to go there, too. In 2019, she was named Best Canadian Author at the Toronto Romance Writers' Northern Hearts Awards for *Until the Last Star Fades*, and her Christmas in London romance, *The Certainty of Chance*, earned a coveted Kirkus starred review and was named by *Entertainment Weekly* as one of the best holiday romances of 2021.

Follow Jacquelyn on Instagram to share her love of books, travel, and pop culture; sign up for her newsletter (www.JacquelynMiddleton. com) for news and contests; and join her drama-free Facebook group (Keeganites United), where members take part in her popular online romance book club, get the inside scoop on advance reader copies, and have the chance to enter exclusive giveaways.

OWN YOUR VOICE

Hope Ellis

"Be yourself; everyone else is already taken." — Oscar Wilde

I'M EARLY IN my writing career. In fact, I'm using "career" far more loosely than say, Stephen King might when considering his vast backlist. When I was invited to contribute to this wonderful compilation, I initially wondered what meaningful advice I could offer to an early or aspiring author. So, I spent time reflecting on my days as pre-published Hope. Naive, starry-eyed Hope, who wanted her "one shot" more than Eminem and Alexander Hamilton combined. I reflected on the events and encounters that surprised me in my publishing journey.

To that end, I'd like to share my hard-earned lessons (ahem, struggles) with preserving my own voice, particularly while writing "own voice" stories.

Be yourself.

There's no way you made it past kindergarten without hearing some version of this well-known aphorism. Whether it's an Oscar Wilde quote or a snappy *Sesame Street* show tune, you likely recognize the undergirding truth. Embracing the eccentricities that make you "different," accepting the quirks that earn you second glances, well, that's what makes you quintessentially *you*. The more I've allowed my inner weirdo tendencies to seep into my writing, the more it's freed my voice. Authenticity is the pixie dust that distinguishes you from a sea of other authors. It also allows other similarly minded reader-weirdos to answer your beacon call. (Yes, there are more of you, and what a happy day it is when you discover your reader tribe.)

I'm a behavioral researcher by day. I have a lifelong love of steamy soap operas, and my friends will testify to my bawdy brand of humor. These facets manifest in my writing as high-heat, "smart" romances in which nerdy characters fall in love. My experiences and perspectives as a black woman often bleed into my characters' motivations. My stories reflect the highs (and hot-ass messiness) I've experienced working in healthcare and academic settings.

I'm very familiar with the topics I write about. Perhaps that's why it was so jarring to have that "authenticity" questioned.

"You can tell people are black by how they talk," someone informed me. "I read your book, and your characters didn't sound black." I don't remember how I responded to that, or similar commentary. I do recall filing it away for consideration. As a researcher, I know data points tell a story. As a new writer, I know feedback is an integral component of the writing process, and a key to improving craft. These observations weren't malicious; in most cases, people were genuinely excited for me. They wanted me to do well, so they were invested in helping me understand how I was, rightly or wrongly, performing blackness.

"What made you pick 'Hope Ellis' as a pen name? It's the most Anglican name I can think of," a consultant said, steering me to pick something more "ethnic." When I decided to address a social justice issue more directly with a black character, complications arose. How would white readers feel about it? They were, after all, potentially a large portion of my readership. What if they didn't like hearing about it? And was the character's concern *really* valid?

Oh oh. A character with a "stereotypically black" name using slang? Did I need to run that by white readers first?

The data points were inconsistent, but the conclusion was clear: There's a right way to write "black." Whether the issue was my failing to write to a stereotype some readers recognized, or creating characters who might be stereotyped, I was doing it wrong.

I know what you're thinking. This is the part of the story where I said, "F*$k that noise," recited Oscar Wilde, and persisted in writing *my* kind of stories.

Nope. Not even close.

This is the part of the story where I dithered back and forth, fighting with myself and all those voices. This is where I grew weary of having to serve as a native informant for some, while fighting to defend my characters and personal identity with others. *This* is when I started to question why I even wanted to write in the first place.

There's all kinds of conversations we could have about these issues. We could talk about standpoint, intersectionality, audience's expectations, writing for universal appeal, etc. In the interests of honesty, we'd also have to acknowledge where these voices come from, and *why* they exist. There's a reason why authors from marginalized groups often have to view "the market" more shrewdly, and employ more tactical approaches to increase their odds of success.

I'm sharing this story because you may one day encounter these voices, especially if you're writing an "own voice" story. Change "black" to any other race, descriptor, or demographic that applies in your case. Should you hear any of these all-knowing voices, I want you to be prepared.

Here's what I found helpful:

Find Your People

With any luck, you've assembled a support team with whom you can share the joys and pains of writing. These folks should challenge your assumptions, push you to grow and say, "F$(k that noise," when necessary. I'm quite lucky, with an unrelentingly supportive circle that includes my publisher, agent, and editors with whom I've built strong relationships, and dear writer friends.

They buoyed my strength when I faltered and helped me push back. They have been invaluable in my journey.

Cultivate Your Audience

As the great philosopher Jay Z once noted, "It ain't for everybody." Neither are you. Internalize this understanding early on and it will save you a great deal of writer angst. Nurture and cultivate your audience. Lean into who you are.

Hold on to Your Joy

Writing is hard work. Stray too far from your reason for writing, from the joy that started you on this path in the first place, and it will feel like a chore. Rest and recharge if you must, but hold on to your joy.

Above all, keep writing! I can't wait to read your work.

Hope Ellis believes romance novels can bring us all closer to world peace. She will never admit that she read her first romance in grade school, but accepts that she's completely addicted now.

Hope is a behavioral health researcher by day and writes sexy romances featuring hot nerds and strong heroines by night. She hopes to one day conquer her habit of compulsively binge-watching *The Office.*

Website: www.hopeellis.com

Instagram: www.instagram.com/ hopeelliswrites

Facebook: www.facebook.com/ hopeelliswrites

Tiktok: www.tiktok.com/@hopeelliswrites

Twitter: https://twitter.com/HopeEllisWrites

WHAT I WISH
I'D KNOWN ABOUT
THIS AUTHOR LIFE ...

Willow Aster

I WISH I'D KNOWN that the writing (my favorite part) is only a small portion of what this career entails.

There's keeping up with social media and ads and changing trends ...

Coming up with teasers and graphics and clever one-liners ...

Mixing things up and staying current ...

Should it be hot-guy abs, sexy-suit hot guy, sweet couples, objects, or illustrated covers?

The place where stories used to reside and frolic around freely is now occupied with all of these things and so much more. And it's really hard not to feel behind all the time, to become a workaholic trying to get it all done, and to beat yourself up when you just can't.

To stay sane and not live in that overwhelmed frame of mind all the time, it's important to stay true to who you are. That doesn't mean you won't change and grow along the way—you absolutely will learn skills you didn't even know you needed—but as long as you're pursuing what you *love*, there are options for almost everything you *don't*.

If your strength is writing and you love to do ads, focus on those things, and hire an assistant or PR team to do the rest. If graphics are your thing and writing is last on your list of loves— I've been surprised by how many authors I've heard say the writing isn't what they love most about this career!—then make killer graphics, write shorter books, and hire an editing team who makes you sound exceptional. In other words, hone in on your strengths and get help with the rest.

At first, you might not make enough money to hire someone, but there's usually a friend or sweet authors out there who are willing to help. Often, a reader that you establish a relationship with will offer to help just to read your book before it releases! And there's always the bartering system. For example, I can edit, but I stink at making graphics, so I'll edit blurbs for my author friends in return for graphics or ad suggestions …

Which leads to this: Take time to establish relationships with people you respect and trust. Not for what it can get you, but *true* friendships. Some of my best friends are people I've met online through this career. It will be those people who get you through the sometimes lonely, confusing, and ever-changing life of being an author.

And because my favorite part is the writing,

I'll add a last thought about that. No matter how many books I publish, I'll always consider myself a student when it comes to the craft. I want to learn and grow continuously, read books about the craft, listen to related podcasts, go to writing conferences, etc., *but* not at the expense of doing the actual writing itself. I'm sure this will be said elsewhere in this book, but it bears repeating because it's just the truth: The best way to become a better writer is to *write* and then write some more and more and more … and then edit, edit, and edit some more.

I wish you well on your writing journey. It's a roller coaster ride, doing this for a living and letting the vulnerability pour out on the page for anyone to read, but there is nothing else in the world I'd rather do. *I love writing.* When you feel that way about it, don't give up. There will be seasons of amazing sales and seasons of lean years, but in all the seasons, try to remember what made you start this in the first place. If it's because you love writing, *period*, your art will always make room for itself.

XO,

Willow

Willow Aster is a *USA Today* bestselling author and lover of anything book-related. She lives in St. Paul, MN with her husband, kids, rescue dog, and grandcat.

Website: www.willowaster.com

Amazon: https://bit.ly/WillowAster

WRITER LIFE

Donna Grant

I GET ASKED A lot about what my typical writing day looks like. For me, routine is key. It is the number one thing that keeps me focused on everything I'm juggling as a writer and owner of my company. And there are a lot of balls I'm keeping in the air at any given time.

It's very easy to spend every hour of my day doing administrative work, writing, or one of the millions of other things that goes into being an author. I'm fortunate enough that writing is my full-time job, so I make sure I use that time wisely. I've learned from bitter experience that I write better in the mornings. I can get out my entire word count for the day before lunch sometimes. That allows me to do other work in the afternoon or take some time to myself.

My routine is simple. My alarm goes off at 6:30, though I *always* hit the snooze at least once. (It's usually twice.) Between my dog and cat, there's no sleeping past seven even if I wanted to. So, after taking the dog out, handing treats to both animals, and feeding the cat, I'm doing yoga. I never feel right when I don't get in some time on the mat.

Then I shower and get ready for the day. That's generally about the time I take the dog for a walk. Then it's breakfast while I give a quick look at any emails that I need to take care of immediately. If they can wait, then I respond after my writing is done.

During my breakfast—and then tea—I do what little I need to do on Facebook. After that, I put everything on Do Not Disturb so I won't get email or text notifications. I write to music, and I prefer headphones, so I put them on, find my writing playlist, and pull up my current work-in-progress. My goal is 20,000 words a week. That breaks down to 4,000 words a day, five days a week. I like my weekends, so I make sure I get my words done during the week. I can write more, but this is a good medium for me. I get what I need down, and I don't feel so drained that I can't write the next day.

I didn't start off writing so many words a day. I began very slowly. I was pregnant with my oldest when I began writing, which meant that my children grew up understanding that I wrote. During their younger years, I wrote when they napped. Over time, I adjusted things based on their ages and schedules. As for how much I wrote, I started with a doable (for me) goal of five pages a day Monday through Friday. I don't know how many words that was. I counted pages back then.

I would write about two books with that

target. Then, I would add a page to my goal with each book. I trained myself to eventually write ten pages a day. Before I knew it, I was at 15. Then 20. I did that for years before I switched to words. It comes out to about the same, in the end. My point is that it's about setting realistic goals to achieve something you can do. Set your aim low, so when you meet it, you feel an accomplishment. You can always add a page (or words) to your goal with your next book.

By training myself, I've always been able to tell my agent or editor exactly how long it would take me to write a book. That is, if there were no issues that crop up like illnesses, Mother Nature, deaths in the family, or divorce.

By taking the weekend off, I can make up a writing day if I get slammed with one of my migraines. Sometimes I do. Sometimes I don't. Because there are occasions when I realize it'll be better if I take those two days off for my mental and emotional wellbeing.

There will always be deadlines in this business. Some we set ourselves, some are set by others. I know I can write ten full books a year. I know because I've done it. But I paid a heavy price for it—and I don't recommend it to anyone. I put my physical, emotional, and mental health into jeopardy. I was drowning in my writing, and I didn't even realize it.

If it wasn't for my children, I don't think I would've left the house. It was that bad. I wasn't exercising, I wasn't eating healthy, and I wasn't listening to what my body was trying to tell me. Even when I was hit with multiple kidney stones in both kidneys at one time that put me in the hospital with various procedures, I still didn't stop. I wrote through all of it. It was an escape. Yet, I should have taken more time for myself to simply rest.

Finding a work-life balance is something authors talk about all the time. We usually joke about our lack of it, but it's a serious business. I've strived for it for years. Then, in January 2020, I decided I was going to spend a year focusing on self-care in a last-ditch effort to try something new. I even dedicated a monthly blog to it so I would be accountable.

This was right before the pandemic first struck. I'm so very thankful I began that trek then, because I'm not sure where I would be if I hadn't. I've continued the journey to this day. I've learned to listen to my soul to give it what it needs. I found yoga and meditation again. When my health was in jeopardy once more, I cut out things that weren't good for me. (I have a cheat day, because I'm only human and my sugar cravings can be detrimental to everyone else's health.)

What I discovered is that when I took time for me, when I listened to my body, I eventually found the balance I'd been reaching for. My work became easier—or as easy as writing can get. I still have difficult books. The ones that are like giving birth. I still have days (weeks!) where I fight for every word on the page.

But at the end of the day, I make sure I take care of myself. Whether that's with a good book, a long soak in the tub, walking my dog to appreciate nature, drinking a glass of wine, or ordering out so I can binge watch something.

Finding ease and balance isn't easy. It's all about discovering what *you* need. It's about listening to your soul. And sometimes it's about making hard decisions that will seem like you're yanked all the way back to the beginning of a difficult road. It's all a process.

If I have any advice to give it's two-fold:

Listen to advice given but take only what works for you.

Trust your heart. It'll never lead you wrong.

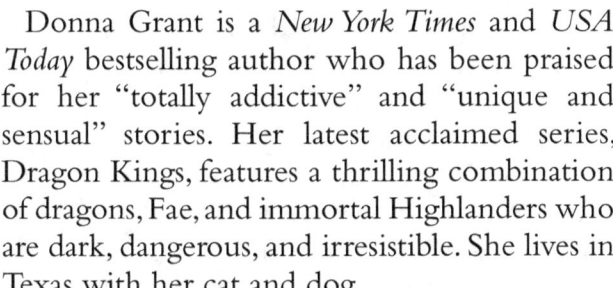

Donna Grant is a *New York Times* and *USA Today* bestselling author who has been praised for her "totally addictive" and "unique and sensual" stories. Her latest acclaimed series, Dragon Kings, features a thrilling combination of dragons, Fae, and immortal Highlanders who are dark, dangerous, and irresistible. She lives in Texas with her cat and dog.

Visit Donna at www.DonnaGrant.com and www.MotherOfDragonsBooks.com

SOCIAL MEDIA:
FB: www.facebook.com/AuthorDonnaGrant

Instagram: www.instagram.com/DGAuthor

Bookbub: www.bookbub.com/authors/
donna-grant

Goodreads: www.goodreads.com/author/
show/1141209.Donna_Grant

Read:
Dragon Eternal
Link: https://dgrant.co/3w1EgIB

Blurb:

In the next installment of her captivating new Dragon Kings series, *New York Times* bestselling author Donna Grant connects an enigmatic and determined Dragon King and a courtesan sent to tempt him to his doom.

He's a man of few words, but she fills his soul with poetry.

Quiet. Brooding. Capable. Shaw's mission is simple: Root out Stonemore's leader and determine what the Divine has in store for the people of Zora and the Kings. Just as he gets started, however, a breathtakingly beautiful woman finds and tempts him like no other. Nothing can stop him from engaging in the pleasures she offers. After all, pillow talk is sometimes the best way to uncover secrets.

Nia's life has never been hers. From starving on the streets to becoming a slave to the Divine, she merely does what's needed to survive. But when her latest assignment brings her face-to-face with a handsome man who makes her feel things she's never experienced before, she begins to see that while she's been living, she's not really thriving.

As truths are revealed, and Nia's blinders are removed, she realizes that she can no longer sit by and allow things to continue as they have been in her city. It's time to take a stand. With Shaw by her side, they spark a war so many have tried to avoid. But the injustices being perpetrated must be stopped—no matter the cost.

THREE THINGS THAT CHANGED MY LIFE AS AN AUTHOR

Amy Mason Doan

SO MUCH OF my writing life is intangible and esoteric that I like to focus on what *is* tangible as much as possible. Becoming an author is a marathon of a mental game, and anything that can help you stay in that game is gold—the same as a gulp of water when you desperately need it, or running shoes that don't give you heel blisters, or a music player that doesn't conk out a mile from the finish line.

Here's my secret—some of the things that changed my life as an author the most are actual, physical *things*. There's loftier-sounding stuff that has helped me—like the conscious decision, after my second novel came out, to excise shame and envy from the publishing process, my commitment to reading extensively both inside and outside of my genre, and my regular, scheduled re-reads of the novels I adored as a girl. Those have kept me going, and kept the joy from going, four books in.

But I value these three things (*things with* a capital *T*) just as much:

1. Try using a timer—this is my best advice for combatting fear. It's device-advice: Try timed writing sessions. I use a burnt orange, analog, KitchenAid egg timer of my mom's from the '70s. I didn't have it when drafting my first novel, *The Summer List*. Doubt crept in with that one—as it inevitably does—but the sustained high of finally writing my first novel after turning 40 was enough to carry me through the tougher sessions. With my second book, *Summer Hours*, I loved the story, but I was really afraid for the first time. *The Summer List* had sold well and gotten good reviews. What if I blew it? What if I only had one good book in me, like the cruel saying goes? What if I could never finish it and had to give my publisher back my advance … or worse, what if I put out something I didn't like?

When I had about 40,000 words (this is the tipping point for me, the mucky middle of the process where it's easy to angst away my time and get stuck), I started setting the burnt-orange KitchenAid for 20 minutes at the beginning of each writing sesh. (I sometimes like to call my writing session a *sesh*, so it sounds less intimidating.) What's 20 minutes? It's so easy, so satisfying to check off of a to-do list. Twenty minutes of writing anything at all and you feel good—in 20 minutes you can get one description of a campfire down on the page, you can tune the voices in one scrap of dialogue.

The burnt-orange KitchenAid timer is permission to accept that not every writing session will be mystical or transportive. Many, sadly, are a grind. But if you put in enough minutes—let's stay away from the scary-sounding "hours"—you'll hit enough highs to keep going.

A lovely thing happened once I started using my timer regularly. I found that after 20 minutes, the fear had subsided. I was back in the story, with my characters coaxing me to go on. Twenty minutes became an hour, then two, then three. That's how books get finished.

2. Get a room divider. An extremely famous writer once said that you should train yourself to work anywhere. That if you can't work in a crowded, noisy room, it's like training a baby to only sleep when the house is dead quiet.

Well, I can't do that. When I'm writing, especially during the dreamy early stages, I can't have people in my sightline making coffee, or putting on socks, or flirting in my sightline when I'm writing, especially during the dreamy early stages. I have an office and a big bedroom in which I can write in pure solitude, but my kitchen nook is sunny and cozy. I fought this for years, and then, during the height of the Covid pandemic, when my family was at home and in my face all day, I bought an accordion-pleated cardboard room divider and closed off the kitchen nook when I was working. It's not fancy, like those Chinoiserie ones you see in old movies. You know, the fancy ones behind which ladies duck behind to change their dresses, and artfully throwing chemises over the top. This isn't that. It was $22.99 and I got it from a dorm-room supply company. (I wish I'd had one back in my college days, so I didn't have to watch my roommate bite her cuticles when I was studying for Anthro midterms, but that's another story ...)

In the winter, I set up a writing nook by the fire, with my feet close to the flames and the cardboard divider behind me. I always leave a little opening for my cat, Leah. She's an approved visitor and likes to check my progress.

3.   Daydream in a hammock. Non-writers envision us sitting at our desks typing, the words pouring from brain to fingertips to screen in one glorious and continual black river. Ha. I stare at the ceiling, scowl at the screen, find excuses to get up and wander around the house. That's what writing usually looks like. Frankly, it's not all that interesting to watch.

One thing that's stayed consistent throughout all of my books is my hammock time. We have this red canvas hammock in our small backyard in Portland, and I think I've come up with my best ideas in there. Maybe the rocking back and forth brings me back to some primal, infant state where I'm less guarded? Maybe it's the fresh air, or the birds calling to each other and bustling around, reminding me that what they're doing is much more important than this story I'm making up in my head.

What I'm trying to say is that daydreaming is part of the process. For me, it's the most important part. I hate the expression "plotter versus pantser," mainly because the word "pantser" sounds like someone who cruises around yanking people's trousers down.

But I guess I'm a plotter. I like to know the ends of my stories before I start. I like to know how I want the reader to *feel* at the end. And I can't figure that out without long days swinging in my hammock, staring up at my magnolia trees—we have this great big wall of camellias in our backyard. That's where I dream up plot twists, where I give my mind empty space in which my characters can wander. That's when they feel most comfortable whispering to me, talking to me, and—if all goes well—when they start to surprise me. My hammock is where I figured out the crucial third-act twist in *The Summer List*, and where I composed the song lyrics, which have secrets hidden in them, for *Lady Sunshine*. And, yea, I've had some delicious, restorative naps cocooned in that hammock …

These three objects aren't beautiful. Well, the hammock used to be, I guess—but now it is faded and the frame is rusty, and we lost the rope-attachment on one side and replaced it with a yellow bungee cord. But they help the magic happen. They help the beauty happen.

And that's the point of this wild, wonderful thing we do, isn't it?

Amy Mason Doan is the bestselling author of *Lady Sunshine*, *The Summer List*, and *Summer Hours*. "Doan's characters leap off the page," says *Publishers Weekly*. "Sure to please fans of Kristin Hannah & Elin Hilderbrand," says *Library Journal*. BookPage describes her work as "an artful combination of lyrical writing and twisting plot."

Amy grew up in Danville, CA and now lives in Portland, OR with her family. Before turning to fiction, Amy worked as a reporter and editor for *The Oregonian, San Francisco Chronicle, Wired, Forbes,* and other publications. Amy has an M.A. in Journalism from Stanford University and a B.A. in English from U.C. Berkeley.

Website: www.amymasondoan.com/

Facebook: www.facebook.com/
amymasondoanauthor

Instagram: www.instagram.com/
amymasondoan/

DEBUNKING TEN PUBLISHING MYTHS

Bob Mayer

MY OPINION IS based on three decades making a living as a writer across the spectrum of traditional, hybrid, indie, Amazon imprint, and hieroglyphic stone cutting. The following are things I hear all the time and I tend to think need to be taken with a small dose of hemlock.

1. "Indie publishing is relatively easy—just get an editor, cover, format and upload."

It takes around three years to learn how to be adept at any profession. That includes self-publishing. There's a reason all those people work at publishing houses. As an indie author, you have to do all their jobs (except editing and cover art). These days, I recommend fiction authors try to get an agent and get traditionally published to start out. Note, I say start out. I believe every traditionally published author needs to become hybrid as soon as possible. You can spend your time learning how to be a better writer or spend it learning to be a publisher. Spend it learning to be a better writer.

2. "My publisher will promote my book."

I had a series that sold over a million copies in paperback for Random House. Every time a new book in the series was scheduled, I'd get all sorts of promises about promotion and then nothing would happen. I finally asked my assigned publicist: "Where do you put all your marketing money?" The reply: "Into our bestsellers." At the time it didn't make sense and seemed unfair. As time has gone by, I get it. They really can't make a bestseller. But once they have one, they can ride that sucker.

It doesn't matter if you're indie, traditionally, or Martian published. You must do the same as far as marketing. What is that? When I teach, I say: "You must market your book. But you can't market your book. But you must. But you can't. But you must. But you can't." Got it? Good. That only took me about a decade, so you're ahead of the power curve.

3. "Authors aren't competing against each other."

This one will get me in trouble, but I hear it all the time. The great brother-, sister-, alienhood of authors. We're all in it together.

First, when a big-time bestseller says it, fine, they can say whatever they want. They're going to sell. Because there are two types of readers. There is the "I need a book, I'm in Costco" type who gets that big-time bestselling author's book. Then there is the prolific reader. That's the audience for all us other authors. And there are only so many of them. And they can only read so fast. So, yeah, we are competing against each other in a tight market.

Does it matter? No. So why bring it up? Because there *are* authors out there who integrate competition in their business plan. And if you don't accept that reality, they can affect your business plan.

Heck, Amazon Marketing Services kind of runs off of that, doesn't it? And if you don't know what that is, back to class.

And because I think authors need to get real and face the fact that this is a brutal business and we're not all standing around the campfire linking arms, although I did do that once with Sue Grafton at Jackson Hole, but that's a story for another day. Rest in peace—a hell of a writer and person. And a realist after coming out of writing television.

4. "Indie book stores are pre-eminent in the industry and we need to support them."

Hell, yeah, I've spent thousands of dollars at indies. As a reader. My experiences as an author are not that great. My motto? Support the indie authors. Yay! How often do you hear that one? How many newspaper articles are written lamenting the career implosion of an indie author? None.

There are lots of great indie bookstores, but there are also a number who are kind of snobbish toward genre authors. Romance authors can tell you about that. On average, over half of the indie stores I've gone into where I've lived (and I've lived a lot of places—they haven't caught me yet) have pretty much given me a cold shoulder since I write genre fiction, not the great American novel.

I've had a couple of experiences where bookstores turned my books away, saying, "We're not interested," only to go under within a year. Lots of wailing and weeping and you know what? I tried to help. Still will.

I had to point out to a friend who was big on the "support your indie, boo to the chains" bandwagon that, in the town I lived in then, his book was racked in the chain, but not in the two indies. Support the place that sells your title.

5. "Getting a Bookbub deal is wonderful."

More controversy. I used to run Bookbub ads constantly, when Bookbub was new. I invested thousands and thousands of dollars, when Bookbub was mainly the province of indie authors. I was in on Bookbub so early I used to be one of the people they suggested you follow when you sign up.

A Bookbub ad would cause a big spike. Then a long tail of nice sales.

Two things happened:

The big spike isn't as big and the long tail is almost gone. I know there are exceptions, but overall a Bookbub ad or a Kindle Daily Deal doesn't have the impact it used to.

Second, New York caught on. Now, the emails are full of bestseller backlist. And remember, it ain't backlist if you haven't read it. So, your prolific reader who you need has a choice between you, the midlist author, and a title from a big-time bestselling author. Tough, eh?

Bookbub is part of the trend of pricing ourselves into oblivion, but we're all guilty of it and it's just a reality. Hell, I'll probably try an ad soon for my new series. There's not much you can do about it, but be aware of the reality.

Here's a key lesson I learned the hard way: Don't joust with windmills. Which leads me to:

6. "Amazon is my enemy."

If you haven't read *The Everything Store*, then you haven't done your homework. Every so often I'll see an author post something on social media tearing into Amazon. Then I'll look up that author on Amazon. And there are the author's books.

Now, I know for traditional authors, they don't control where their books are placed, but I assure you, no one is giving back the money coming in from Amazon. Amazon is a reality of the business. They own the e-book market. And 30 percent at least of the print, probably more. Is that correct? Is it fair? That's a different matter.

Factor Amazon into your business plan. Use it. But also remember that another myth is .....

7. "Amazon is my friend."

Amazon will screw you if it makes the business decision to change something. It's not like they picked you specifically. They just made a business decision. You know, like Denzel Washington in *Man on Fire*. It's just business.

I have so many titles on Amazon I can literally see when the algorithms change based on what happens to my sales.

When they did away with Kindle Worlds with two weeks' notice, it devastated some authors who were making a nice living in that niche. If they decide to change royalty rates, they'll do it and they don't care whether I, Bob Mayer, like it or not. So, I always keep a wary eye on what Amazon is doing.

Not only is Amazon not your friend, I will extend that to ...

8. "My agent, editor, publisher, etc., is my friend."

I see writers say, "I love my agent."

That's cool. There are agents I have tremendous respect for and think are great people. Same with editors. But when it's a business arrangement, it's a business arrangement. Sort of like marriage. The love can go out the window fast when the numbers don't add up.

That being said, the biggest mistake I made as a writer is …

9. "I can make a living from home and not have to network."

You and one other person. I think his name is Stephen. Last name King. For the rest of us, networking is critical. Conferences and cons aren't for parties. They're for networking and making friends, even though we're competing against each other and your agent isn't your friend, but yeah, she is. Kind of.

Which leads me to the worst myth:

10. "It's impossible to make a living as a writer."

You'll hear that one lamented in the halls of MFA programs everywhere. You'll hear it from authors who "failed." You'll hear how they got screwed by their agent (who, apparently, didn't love them back), their editor, their publisher, the bookstores, the readers, yada yada yada.

But you know what? There are a lot more people making a living writing than you realize. Most of them are flying low, under the radar, because they're busy *writing*.

I firmly believe now, this moment, is the best time ever to be a writer. Why? Because you control your destiny. The only thing between you and the reader is the internet. The only person who can say no to your career is you. The only person who can make you quit is you.

Trust me. I'm your friend and not competing with you.

Bob Mayer grew up in New York City and is a *New York Times* bestselling author and graduate of West Point. He's had over 80 books published and sold over five million, including the #1 series The Green Berets, Shadow Warriors, Area 51, Atlantis, and the Time Patrol. Download his free Readers Guide for a list of all his titles and links at www.bobmayer.com.

Instagram: www.instagram.com/sifiauthor/

Facebook: www.facebook.com/ authorbobmayer

Twitter: https://twitter.com/Bob_Mayer

Books to Buy:

Writer's Little Black Book: Problems, Solutions and Advice To Help Write, Publish and Profit The Novel Writers Toolkit

Write it Forward: From Writer to Successful Author

GET YOURSELF A WRITER'S ROOM

Laurelin Paige

AS YOUNG WRITERS, we're all very protective of our baby ideas. We huddle over them and nurture them like they're eggs in our nest—eggs that only we can hatch properly before sending them, freshly written, flying off to critique partners and editors. It's a lovely, lonely process. I used it myself for untold books before finally, almost accidentally, discovering the trick Hollywood has known about for ages—the writer's room.

In case you aren't familiar, the writer's room is how your favorite shows are written. One person comes in with the idea, and then the others bounce it around, expanding and editing, until it's polished.

I'm not suggesting you team up with all your friends to write your book—although having done that, I can say it's also lots of fun. Instead, use your own personal writer's room instead of a single plot partner. Get together, in person or on a call, everyone together. (Taking "plot walks" with friends is one of my favorite variations of this.) This is key to the magic: You can't go through your people one at a time. The group dynamic is what makes the process so effective. Go through your plot, start to finish. If you aren't an outliner, chances are that you still know what major plot points need to happen in order for your characters to successfully complete their emotional journeys.

It's not a fast process. You might find it takes an hour, or three hours. But that commitment to time up front will save you days, or even weeks, of rewrites later. Your story will be stronger and you'll write faster as a result of having a tight plot.

I can't tell you the number of times I've been saved by discovering in advance of writing that I was headed in the wrong direction, missing a thread, or contradicting my earlier work in the universe. My time, as is everyone's, is worth money. Losing a week's worth of words is the equivalent of losing a week's pay, and that doesn't even account for missing deadlines, moving edits, etc. With a writer's room, I can be confident about sticking to my schedule.

Easy peasy, right? There is one small catch. The effectiveness of your personal writer's room hinges completely on the types of people you invite in. I've found, through using the Clifton Strengths, three invaluable archetypes for this work.

First, an idea person. Now, as writers, we're

sort of all idea people, aren't we? However, someone who has ideation as a top strength will be able to pivot instantly, offering lots of choices when you're stuck. And you will get stuck, because you're also going to want a detail-oriented person on your team. They'll find all the plot holes you've overlooked— and we all overlook them right up until we've written ourselves into a corner. Finally, a deep thinker can help you sift past the exciting plot points and down into the heart of the story: the why's and the wounds that power the plot.

It's not an easy task to take all your fledgling ideas and pour them out in front of people, especially when you know they'll tear some of them apart. But just like with children, I'm finding more and more that it takes a village to raise my ideas from sparks to completion with the least amount of angst on my end. After all, we need our characters to suffer—not ourselves.

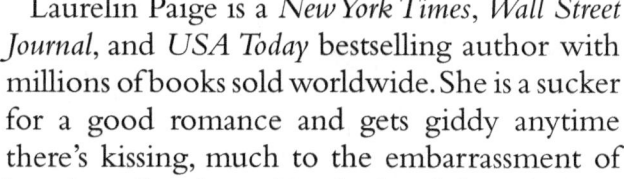

Laurelin Paige is a *New York Times*, *Wall Street Journal*, and *USA Today* bestselling author with millions of books sold worldwide. She is a sucker for a good romance and gets giddy anytime there's kissing, much to the embarrassment of her three daughters. Her husband doesn't seem to complain, however.

When she isn't reading or writing sexy stories, she's probably singing, watching *Killing Eve* or *Letterkenny*, or dreaming of Michael Fassbender. She's also a proud member of

Mensa International, though she doesn't do anything with the organization except use it as material for her bio.

She is represented by Rebecca Friedman. Find her books and reading order at her website, *https://laurelinpaige.com.*

Amazon: www.amazon.com/Laurelin-Paige/e/B00CR6KMWQ

BookBub: www.bookbub.com/authors/laurelin-paige

Facebook: www.facebook.com/LaurelinPaige/

Facebook reader group (Laurelin Paige's Sky Launch) https://www.facebook.com/groups/HudsonPierce/

Goodreads: www.goodreads.com/laurelinpaige

Instagram: www.instagram.com/thereallaurelinpaige/

Pinterest: www.pinterest.com/LaurelinPaige/_created/

Spotify: https://open.spotify.com/user/1290070318

TikTok: www.tiktok.com/@laurelinpaige

NINETEEN THINGS YOU CAN DO TO HELP SELL YOUR BOOK

Zibby Owens

CONGRATULATIONS! YOU SOLD your book! You probably just jumped up and down in excitement. (I know I did when my memoir sold after almost 20 years.) But wait. There's a little something else you should probably know. Sit down. Ready?

You've just accepted an entirely new job. Surprise! Yes, first and foremost, you're a writer. But if you'd like anyone to read those beautiful pages, you're also now a professional marketer. And your product is words.

What's that? You don't know how to do marketing? Well, buckle up. You don't have a choice.

When my first anthology came out, I walked into many bookstores expecting to proudly see it on the shelves. The first few stores didn't even carry it. One said they'd had two copies but sold them and weren't reordering. (Why?!) Another pointed me to a section I didn't think represented the book and I found one lone copy on a super high shelf. How would anyone ever discover it in a bookstore to buy it? Answer: They wouldn't. I realized then that I had to sell readers on my books long before they stepped foot in most bookstores. But how?

Here are a few tips.

Start thinking about yourself as a brand. Spend five minutes brainstorming a few characteristics that describe your author brand. Accessible? Ultra-literary? Warm? Aspirational? Approachable? If you were a food or an item of clothing, what would you be and why? Imagine what you want your readers to think and feel about you after reading your book. Keep those bullet points close.

Commission a logo and an author website. Don't know how? Hire a Squarespace expert, look for someone on Publishers Marketplace, or just Google it. Launch a contest on *99designs. com*. Make sure your website and logo convey the same feel as your overall brand.

Craft a social media identity. Just posting pictures of your cat? Not anymore. Make an easy-to-guess username. If your name is Jane Smith, try to get @janesmithauthor or @byjanesmith or something that other people can guess. (I tag people when I recommend books and if I can't figure it out after five tries, I give up.) Try to use the same username across all platforms. Join Instagram, Facebook, Twitter, TikTok, Goodreads, and LinkedIn. Be consistent. Use the same photo in your profile and the same description for all of them. "Jane Smith writes warm, approachable love stories. Mostly, she loves her cat."

Get some professional photos taken of yourself. I didn't know why people suggested I do this, but I listened. I hired a photographer early on. Four years later, I've used all of those pictures 1,000 times. Even grab a friend with a great iPhone. Spend two hours together. Change your outfit about eight times. Pose reading a book. Writing. Casual. Standing up. Sitting down. At your favorite bookstore. On the street. With your family. Without. You will end up using these!

Start posting on social media early. Show your followers the behind-the-scenes of your publishing journey. Post pictures of where you write, places that inspired you, books you love that are aligned with your brand, your routine, your favorite bookstores, and, if you feel comfortable, other people and things in your life. Even your cat. Remember that posting on social media is writing. I view it as my daily writing exercise. It's immediate and a great litmus test for what's resonating with your audience. I posted about staying home with my kids for 11 years before going back to work full-time and women went crazy. Who knew!? This is your greatest marketing tool that you get to hone every day.

Connect with other writers. Befriend them on social media. Join Facebook groups. Go to author events. Join a conference. Ask your publisher to introduce you to others in your imprint. Just start making author friends. It's so important to have a community of people who understand you and also whose books you can help promote and they can help you, too. Don't feel like an impostor. You're a writer. Connect, connect, connect.

Form relationships at the indie bookstores you love. You probably already have them. (I used to babysit the kids of my favorite bookstore owner years ago!) Visit often. Volunteer to moderate events. Support the bookstore by tagging them on social media, visiting often, doing events, and spending time in the store. It will help when your book comes out to have an advocate in the store who might just put your book on the front table.

Figure out who your audience is and where they are. What else do they like? Where can you find them? Later, you may need to use this information for creative event venues and partnerships.

Work with your publisher early to determine what their marketing plan will be. And then, augment it. No one will be thinking about your book more than you. What can you do to help? Do you know a local store owner in your hometown who could sell your book or host an event for you? Are they planning on taking social media ads? If not, you should consider doing some boosted posts as you build up your followers.

Think about publicity. Who do you know or

who can you be introduced to at any media outlets? You might want to hire your own publicist. They are expensive and the results are often disappointing, but it's usually worth it. Media outlets (which I also am!) get pitched hundreds of books a week. But I do pay attention to the publicists I'm used to working with when they send me a new book versus a cold pitch from an unknown author. Ask friends to introduce you via email to anyone who could be remotely helpful.

Hone your message early. What is your book about? What inspired you to write it? What's your writing process like? Sit down and write out answers to these questions and any others you can think of. Then, memorize the answers. Don't get caught off guard by any questions from the media, friends, bookstore owners, or colleagues. You're a writer. Write the answers. Then practice saying them over and over again. By the time the book comes out and you start doing podcast interviews, you should be a total pro.

Think about other ways to hone your brand. Maybe you want to start a podcast like I did. Maybe you want to blog. Maybe you want to teach classes or start a book club or something. It won't hurt.

Don't forget real life. Covid has made planning a joke (we plan, God laughs) but it's still worth doing. Host events at home or at bookstores. Meet up with people. Get out there. But don't ever bring galley or advanced reader copies of your book and hand them to the media or other authors at parties, particularly not at another authors' book reading! Just ask if you can send a copy and follow-up later. Don't be pushy. Be respectful and subtle. You have a prized package. It shouldn't be thrown in someone's face like a sidewalk vendor waving a flier.

When you send someone an advance copy of your book, include a handwritten note. Try to include something clever tied to the book, but you don't have to go crazy. A printed bookmark. A notepad. A pen. Think about something the gift receiver might be able to use and might not throw away! Then always make sure to follow-up. They might not have received it.

Plan a pub day event for friends and family involving an indie bookstore. Try to book as many indie bookstore events as you can, but also other types like stores, religious institutions, and schools. Buy a few sharpies and bring them with you to signings. Maybe bring those clever bookmarks you printed (see above) for the audience.

Try not to get caught up in the numbers. When the book comes out, a lot of focus externally will be on sales. You'll be able to see the NPD Bookscan number of how many books you sold each week by starting an author.amazon.com account. The numbers will almost definitely be disappointing. There are so, so many books that come out every year and who has time to read?! No reader is sitting there wishing for your book. So everyone who does read it is a gift. Don't lose sight of why you wrote this book to begin with. It wasn't for a certain number of readers. It was to get your thoughts and creative message into the world. To connect with readers. (If you wanted to do something for the money, it wouldn't be book publishing.) You're doing it. You did it. It's like magic: Your thoughts in someone else's head. Take a moment to celebrate the win. The achievement. Don't forget who you are and how it all started.

Start writing your next book. You always want to have an answer to, "What's coming next for you?" and it shouldn't be spending more time with your cat. Get back to the words. The thoughts. The empty pages.

Just say yes. Yes to a new idea. Yes to an event invitation. Yes to a podcast. Yes to an author meet-up. Yes to all of it. Who knows where life will take you? In this moment, be all in.

Keep reading. Keep promoting your friends' books. Keep losing yourself in stories. There's no better time than during the stress of book promotion to get lost in someone else's story and to remember the power of reading. That's why we do all of this, right? So grab a cup of coffee, pick up a novel or a memoir or a thriller or a poetry collection, something that moves you, crack open the spine, and snuggle up with your cat. Just don't forget to post about it.

Zibby Owens is the award-winning creator and host of the popular literary podcast Moms Don't Have Time to Read Books, which spawned a media company. Zibby Owens Media includes the Zcast podcast network, the Zibby Books publishing company, and the Moms Don't Have Time To brand.

She is the editor of two anthologies, *Moms Don't Have Time To: A Quarantine Anthology* and *Moms Don't Have Time to Have Kids: A Timeless Anthology*; a children's book, *Princess Charming*; and a memoir, *Bookends: A Memoir of Love, Loss, and Literature*. You can find her at zibbyowens.com and on social media @zibbyowens.

ADVICE FOR ASPIRING WRITERS

JoAnn Ross

IBELIEVE THAT THE most important advice for both aspiring and published authors is credited to Somerset Maugham. When asked by a student in his English literature class how to write a novel, he replied: "There are three rules for the writing of a novel. Unfortunately, no one knows what they are."

Obviously, publishing requires a knowledge of grammar and craft. Those are the basics. But after that, you must learn by trial and error what works for you. Even then, over time your process will undoubtedly change. I've written more than a hundred books over 39 years, and my process these days in no way resembles the way I wrote in the 1980s.

Once you get the basics down, I believe that passion and persistence are the two most important things all writers must possess. It's passion for storytelling that drives us to write, study our craft, and keep writing even during difficult times. It's our passion for our stories that shine through, captures readers' attention, and makes people we'll probably never meet want to read them. Conversely, a lack of passion will also show in our work. If we don't have a burning passion for storytelling, how can we expect anyone else be moved by what we write?

Then there's persistence. I always advise aspiring writers not to allow themselves to stop writing when a story isn't working. This usually occurs during the middle—or what I refer to as the muddle—of a story. This is when it's tempting to chase after that new and shiny idea shimmering in our minds. When the writing gets tough, the tough keep writing.

That said, if you're meant to be a writer, the ideas will come. If staring at a blank screen or page creates anxiety rather than words, allow yourself to take a break. Go weed a garden, paint a wall, bake bread, read a book outside your genre, take a walk, watch a sunset. When your mind is relaxed and open, ideas will come.

There's an apocryphal story that blends both passion and persistence that has always appealed to me. There's a young musician who, after years of study and practice, finally got an opportunity to have his work judged by a world-famous maestro who told him that he'd never have a career in music because he had no fire.

The young man was understandably crushed. But he got over his disappointment eventually; he went on to have a nice career outside of music, married, and had a family he loved very much. Many years later, the maestro, who was by now a very old man, returned to town to play a concert engagement.

After the performance, the man went backstage, introduced himself again, and said, "Years ago I was hoping to live my dream of being a violinist, but when I played for you, you said I had no fire. I've gone on to have a good life, a wonderful family, and a successful career. But I've always wondered, how could you tell, in that brief time, that I'd never play professionally?"

The old man shrugged. "I tell that to all young musicians," he said. "If you'd truly had the fire, nothing I could've said would have stopped you from fulfilling your dream."

Keep your eye on the prize, keep the passion burning, hold fast to your dream, and don't let anyone stop you from writing. And never, ever, forget that to achieve the incredible, you have to attempt the impossible.

JoAnn Ross is the *New York Times* and *USA Today* bestselling author of over 100 novels published in 27 countries. Two of her titles have been excerpted in *Cosmopolitan* magazine and her books have also been published by the Doubleday, Rhapsody, Literary Guild, and Mystery Guild book clubs. She lives with her husband and rescued Siamese cat,

The Dowager Empress Paws—who pretty much rules the house—in her beloved Pacific Northwest.

www.joannross.com

www.facebook.com/JoAnnRossbooks

instagram.com/joannrossbooks

www.bookbub.com/authors/joann-ross

WRITE THE BOOK

Bella Matthews

IN JULY 2020, while the world was on lockdown, I ordered a new MacBook, thinking I'd start a podcast so I could tell the world about my love of all things romance books. I'd been reading and reviewing romance on my Instagram account for years and thought that might be the next logical step. But when my shiny, new—albeit slightly used and refurbished—laptop was finally in my hands and all my sparkly new apps were loaded, instead of looking into what I needed for a podcast, I opened Word.

By the end of the day, I'd written the first six chapters of what would eventually become my very first book, *All In*.

I never looked back.

Two years later, that book ended up being the first in a series. I now have nine book babies out in the world and at least two more up for pre-order, as well as stacks of notebooks full of carefully jotted down ideas for what I plan to write over the next three years. If I don't write those babies down when they hit me, I'll forget them before it's time to let those characters speak.

As a newbie in this crazy author world, I'm often asked what advice I'd give other aspiring authors.

My answer is always the same three words: Write the book.

So many things go into being a successful author, and yes, they're all important. There's editing, cover designs, marketing, and social media, just to name a few. It's easy to become so tangled up in all these ancillary things you think you need to know or do before you can publish your book that you trip and fall and give up completely before you even start.

Don't worry about all the things that come after.

Just write the book you want to write.

Put pen to paper, or more likely, put your fingers on those keys and write.

Don't have a ton of alone time to start? Write at night after you put the kids to bed. Too tired to write after your long day of working your existing job? Because the reality is yes, most of us already have a forty-hour-a-week job before, during, and after we publish our first book. I sympathize with you. Write in the mornings before everyone gets out of bed. Write on the weekends with a big cup of coffee sitting next to you, or bring your laptop and a glass of wine to your favorite comfy spot in your house later in the day. Hey, it's five o'clock somewhere. The key here is to be one with Nike and "Just do it."

Write.

Editors, cover designers, and all the other things you'll have to figure out to publish your book won't matter if you don't have a book written. Truthfully, it's remarkably easy to come up with excuse after excuse about why we don't have the time or the money to publish. But before you worry about any of that, you need to write the book.

Without question, writers face a steep learning curve to becoming a self-published author. I've found, however, that most people are more than happy to answer your questions, and social media can be a wonderful tool to help you connect with other people who are going through—or have already been through—what you're doing. But before you stress about whether your book is good enough, or your cover is on point, or even when the perfect release date is, experience how incredibly rewarding it is to type "The End."

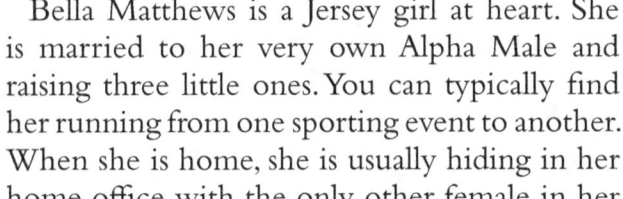

Bella Matthews is a Jersey girl at heart. She is married to her very own Alpha Male and raising three little ones. You can typically find her running from one sporting event to another. When she is home, she is usually hiding in her home office with the only other female in her house, her rescue dog Tinker Bell by her side.

She likes to write swoon-worthy heroes and sassy, smart heroines with a healthy dose of laughter and all the feels.

Website: www.authorbellamatthews.com/

Facebook: www.facebook.com/Bella.
Matthews.Author

Instagram: www.instagram.com/
bellamatthews.author/

Tiktok: www.tiktok.com/@
bellamatthewsauthor

WHAT I WISH I KNEW ...

Melanie Summers

A
S OBVIOUS AS it sounds, I wish I'd known you can't please everyone. There is no such thing as a perfect book, nor one that will be loved universally. Need some convincing? Look up *Pride and Prejudice* on Goodreads and read some of the nearly 90,000 one-star reviews.

When I put out my first book, I fooled myself into thinking that it was so magically delicious that no one could possibly resist it. It was for *anyone* who loves romance (and would even be enjoyed by those who don't read the genre, because it was *that* good). Go ahead and laugh. It's damn funny.

About five days after I hit the publish button, I got my first one-star review. For over a week, I took it with me everywhere, letting it hang over me like a dark cloud, stealing my thunder the entire time (even though the book was selling really freaking well and was getting a whole lot of five-star reviews). Then it hit me: If was going to do this whole author thing, I needed to find a way to reconcile with the fact that I was going to get crappy reviews. It's not an "if," it's a "when" thing. And if I wasted a week or so each time someone gave me a bad review, that was going to add up fast to one mostly miserable life.

That's when I came up with my mango or papaya analogy (which is adapted from some sage dating advice I'd seen on some TV show I can't remember).

So here goes:

I love papayas. Love 'em. I would eat them every day if I could. My husband, however, passes on papayas, but he enjoys mangoes (which taste like soap to me). My books might taste like soap to someone, but it doesn't mean that person has poor taste in books *or* that my book is bad (and therefore I'm the world's worst writer). My book just isn't for that reader. And that's okay.

Remember the mangoes and papayas when you get a bad review. Hopefully, it will help you shake it off quickly.

But if that doesn't work for you, think of reviews this way: They are none of your business. True story. Reviews are written for other readers. Since I don't need to read reviews to know whether I'd like my own books, those reviews clearly weren't written for me. This also means I don't have any need to "go after a reviewer" for writing something negative about my book. Some writers go down that rabbit hole and, if you remember nothing else from what I'm writing here, remember this: *Do not respond to bad reviews*. Don't waste your valuable time begging Amazon to take the review down. (They won't unless it's an extreme situation, like the review is suggesting the author be murdered or something.) Don't mobilize a group of fans to go on the attack. Trust me, no good can come of it. Spreading hate about a reviewer only leads to more hate (because reviewers have friends, too). Just tell yourself, "They must like mangoes," and move on with your day.

And by move on with your day, I mean focus on finding the people who *will* love your work and figure out how to consistently please them. Conjure up your ideal reader, ask yourself what she needs when she opens your book, then give it to her. Make a promise and keep it.

I started out with steamy romance, then moved to rom-coms. My books are on the longer side, so even my steamy romances hit a certain demographic. What I've come to understand about my readers is they are generally college grads, most are moms ages 34-59, and a majority of them also work full-time outside the home. They don't usually have time to read during the week, but they make time for it on the weekends. They are looking for an escape from the world—something light, heartwarming, funny, and romantic. So when I start each novel, I start it with a promise to my reader: This book will be light, funny, romantic, and heartwarming. In fact, my author tagline is: "Laugh. Feel Good. Fall in Love." My covers convey the same message, as do my blurbs, my Instagram and Facebook posts, and my newsletters. They all say: This will be fun!

Keeping that message the same across the board has helped me find *my* readers—the ones who I can please. Once I found them, I've done my level best to keep my promise to them (not to every reader out there), because that's the deal we've made. They'll buy my books and I'll deliver what I've said I will—a nice, ripe, juicy papaya.

Melanie Summers made a name for herself with her debut novel, *Break in Two*, a contemporary romance that cracked the Top 10 Paid on Amazon in both the UK and Canada, and the Top 50 Paid in the USA. Her highly acclaimed Full Hearts Series was picked up by both Piatkus Entice (a division of Hachette UK) and HarperCollins Canada. Her first three books have been translated into Czech and Slovak by EuroMedia. Since 2013, she has written and published eleven novels and three novellas. She has sold over a quarter of a million books around the globe.

In her previous life (i.e. before having children), Melanie got her Bachelor of Science from the University of Alberta, then went on to work in the soul-sucking customer service industry for a large cellular network provider that shall remain nameless (unless you write her personally—then she'll dish). On her days off, she took courses and studied to become a Chartered Mediator. That designation landed her a job at the R.C.M.P. as the Alternative Dispute Resolution Coordinator for "K" Division. Having had enough of mediating arguments between gun-toting police officers, she decided it was much safer to have children so she could continue her study of conflict in a weapon-free environment (and one which doesn't require makeup and/or nylons).

Melanie resides in Edmonton with her husband, their three kiddos, one adorable but neurotic no-eyed dog, Lucy, and a small furry dictator named Nelson. When she's not writing novels, Melanie loves reading (obviously), snuggling up on the couch with her family for movie night (which would not be complete without lots of popcorn and milkshakes), and long walks in the woods near her house. She also spends a lot more time thinking about doing yoga than actually doing yoga, which is why most of her photos are taken "from above." She also loves shutting down restaurants with her girlfriends. Well, not literally shutting them down, like calling the health inspector or something—more like just staying until they turn the lights off.

Website: www.melaniesummersbooks.com/home

Tiktok: www.tiktok.com/@melaniesummers

Instagram: www.instagram.com/mj_summers_
author/

Facebook: www.facebook.com/

MJSum https://twitter.com/
MJSummersBooksmersAuthorPage

Twitter: https://twitter.com/
MJSummersBooks

A PROFESSIONAL WRITER WRITES ... NO MATTER WHAT

Mary Leo

I'VE BEEN PUBLISHED since 2004 when my first book hit the bookshelves. At the time, my husband and I had only recently moved to a small town in central Pennsylvania and finding a bookstore to check out my first novel on a shelf ended up being a task in itself. We eventually found an independent bookstore located inside a sparsely populated mall and, low and behold, there was my book, *Stick Shift*, all two copies, sitting on the shelf with hundreds of other books.

I thought I'd do a happy dance, bells and horns would go off, the store owner would come over to congratulate me, people would clamor for my autograph, I'd want to hoot and holler, or at the very least feel some grand emotion. After all, it had taken me years of learning my craft, scores of writing classes, and numerous workshops, along with writing and rewriting books that never saw the light of day, to get me there. Then there was the whole rejection cycle by countless agents and editors. Surely, I would feel delighted to see the end product of all my hard work.

Instead, I spotted the book, spine out, slipped it from its entrapment, showed my husband who seemed more excited about it than I was, shoved it back onto the shelf and thought … *is that all there is?*

Believe me, most authors don't think this way when they see their first book on a shelf in a bookstore. They are, in fact, excited.

Since then, I've learned that getting your book published in any form on any site or in any bookstore is an amazing accomplishment in itself. No need for bright lights or screaming fans. It's one of those moments in life when you say to yourself, *I did that.* I took my gift of writing, created a story, and had it published. The secret is, once you've accomplished this incredible task, you should physically pat yourself on the back, celebrate the moment, and write the next book.

But here's the thing about this writing gift: Unless you value it, nurture it, guard it, and share that gift with others, it can easily fade away. It can bury itself so deep, you may think you've lost it or can't do it anymore, or it simply disappeared. Perhaps you've even run out of story ideas. You no longer have the time, the skill, or worst of all … you've come to believe nobody cares to read your books.

Unfortunately, I've witnessed this firsthand way too many times from authors who are brilliant in what they do, but have allowed limiting beliefs to not only take hold, but to permanently move in and cast off any contrary positive thoughts.

Are you one of them?

You may spend days, weeks, months, or even years fermenting in these ill-begotten notions, going so far as to seek professional help, only to be told that yes, you poor suffering writer, you've lost your writing mojo and it's a long, bleak road back ... if you ever get there at all.

I'm here to tell you: *Bullshit!*

For whatever reason, you've allowed your self-doubting, fear mongering, and limiting-belief critic to drill into your thoughts and take root ... Resist at all costs!

That's when a beautiful golden light threatens to go out. That's when a reader who needs the story only you can write is denied the amazing gift of your words, because you, as a creative artist, have allowed a negative pattern to destroy your personal treasure. No one else, no matter how talented, can write your stories. No one else has your voice, your way of seeing the world, or your special gift of words.

Oh, but I'm really blocked, you might say. *I'm totally burned out. I'm too sad, too tired, too sick.* Or even worse ... *I've tried, but I can't make this career work and I'm afraid to try again.*

All valid thoughts, but is that how you want to treat this amazing gift you've been given?

The gift that's always with you, that you've had since forever; the gift you toyed with and discovered you could do for hours when you're in the flow? The gift that brings you countless hours of joy, and fills your life with a myriad of imaginary friends, situations, fascinating places, love, hate, fear, and makes your heart pound?

I know you can revive that passion, that lust, that incredible drive to tell a story, even when you've filled your day with so many other commitments, there simply isn't any time to write. I've been there … I've done that … and I've learned how to step over all that limiting crap.

You can, too.

Deep in your heart, you know there's always time to write. You know you can grab fifteen minutes before dinner, a half hour in the early morning or during lunch, or even an entire hour at night before bed. Plus, you also know that you haven't been nurturing your gift, cherishing it, enjoying all that it has to share with you. This dismissal of your gift has caused the people around you to believe you no longer care about your writing. It's given them permission to fill your time with their needs, and you've allowed it to happen.

Here's the thing, and I don't say this lightly, you've participated in your own creative demise, and perhaps at times, even encouraged it. You've allowed yourself to experience all these negative thoughts about your writing, and perhaps even indulged in the benefits of hanging with folks who feel the same way.

As Tony Robbins says, we can change our mindset in the snap of our fingers.

We can choose to be protective of our writing. To feel the joy once again. To snatch fifteen minutes here or an hour there just to indulge ourselves and write.

A professional writer writes … no matter what.

What separates a professional writer from everybody else is that a professional writer writes despite what's going on around them. Despite all the noise. Despite all the self-doubt. And despite not being in the mood.

I lost my darling husband a few years ago, and despite that tragic loss, I somehow continued to write and prosper. During those hours of immersed fantasy, I wasn't sobbing, wasn't feeling the despair, the hurt, the terrible loss, the wretched sadness that emanates from somewhere deep in my soul. My writing helps me get through the worst of times, and I'm blessed because of it.

It's said that Alexander Solzhenitsyn wrote while in the Russian Gulag. Talk about not being in the mood, or being under duress, or having the wrong environment … he wrote anyway.

If you have to dance, sing, jump, scream, run, walk, work out, take a shower, or even eat a cupcake before you write, do it. If you have to wear a hat, a shawl, a crown, a wig, a Spider-Man costume, or your favorite torn shirt, wear it. If the story needs to be all plotted out with spreadsheets and templates, create them. If the story comes to you as you write, embrace it. If you like quiet, music, rain, the sound of a crowded café, cars driving past, waves, or children playing, make it happen. If you like to stand, sit, walk, or jog while you're writing, do it. If you like to type, dictate, use a ballpoint pen, a feather pen, a pencil, a colored marker, or a chunk of coal to write, use it. If you like to write alone at a desk, in a bed, on the sofa, a recliner, a chase by the pool, find a way to do it. If you like to write with a group, in a park, in a church, or in a busy hotel lobby, go there. If you need an accountability coach, a counselor, a friend texting you, a cat in your lap, your dog by your side, or a parrot on a perch, make it happen.

Whatever you think holds you back, take the uncomfortable action to change that barrier. Do whatever it takes to make the words happen.

And remember … there's a reader who is looking for your next book. That reader will never find your story if you don't write it.

You're a writer. No matter where you are in your journey, once you recognize your gift, embrace it. What separates a professional writer from everybody else is that a professional writer writes … no matter what.

Now go write.

It's what we do.

Mary Leo is a *USA Today* bestselling author who has had a successful writing career for nearly 20 years. During that time, she has been continuously published in the romance genre, both traditionally and independently. Her books have been translated into several different languages, and have hit #1 in her Amazon categories.

Mary truly believes that when a writer stops writing, for whatever reason, a light goes out, and there isn't another light to take its place. Each writer has a unique voice, a unique way to see the world, and no one else, no matter how talented, can replace that gift. She's on a mission to help writers start writing again, to finish their projects, to publish their books, and to once again serve humanity with their very special gift. She has helped fellow writers to turn their unique light back on and to keep it burning bright despite setbacks and limiting beliefs.

Website: www.maryleo.com/

Facebook: www.facebook.com/
maryleoauthor/

Twitter: https://twitter.com/maryleoauthor

Instagram: www.instagram.com/
maryleoauthor/

IMPORTANT TRUTHS
FOR WRITERS

Jen Talty

I T'S HARD FOR me to believe that I began my journey as a writer nearly twenty years ago. I was 37 years old and I wrote my first manuscript long-hand. Actually, I wrote the first four of them that way. I didn't have a laptop, so wherever I was with my kids, watching their sports practices, I'd take pen to paper and craft my story, only to sit late at night at the kitchen desk and type my story onto the computer.

This was back in 2003 and publishing looked quite different than it does now. Indie publishing wasn't something a *real* writer would ever consider. Going with a small *digital* publisher looked as though the author was *desperate* to be published.

Facebook was barely a thing. I remember being told Myspace was all the rage.

When I look back, I remember how utterly overwhelmed I was at everything I had to learn. Until I went to my first Romance Writers of

America local chapter meeting, I had no idea about the world of publishing and what it took to become a successful author. I sat there and listened to the seasoned authors and was overwhelmed with the chatter about craft and the authors using terms I had never heard of. It got worse when they moved onto topics regarding agents and publishing contracts. I felt out of place and was unsure if I even wanted to jump into this world at all.

But I had written a book and I wanted to make it better. I wanted to learn. I opened my ears and listened. I took notes and I asked questions about craft. I figured I'd deal with how to get it published later because no one was going to take me seriously if I didn't write a better book.

I was lucky. The group I joined had over fifty members and more than half were seasoned, published authors. A small group had agents and were well on their way to becoming published. They took me under their wing and guided me through a maze that there was no way I could have navigated on my own. They held my hand at conferences. Again when rejection letters came. And they were there when I finally got "the call."

They helped me understand the contract with the publisher and later with my agent. They helped me when it was time for me to leave my first agent and when my publisher went bankrupt. Without the support of my fellow authors, I would not have ever been published, much less published more than 50 books.

Publishing may look different. And it might have changed. And it will change again. However, the idea of authors supporting authors and guiding each other through the process is one that is necessary.

Writing is a lonely business. We sit in our office, alone, writing about people that don't exist.

Becoming a successful author means understanding two things.

The craft of writing.

And the business of publishing.

Honing our skills as a writer should be priority number one. Crafting that better book takes precedence. Becoming complacent in this area would most definitely mean the end of a career. Discussing plot, character, and other writerly things with our fellow authors is a real treat. Going to professional conferences and attending workshops, even when we think we already know the topic, sometimes sparks those creative juices and gives us that push we've been looking for, or we meet a new writer that offers us the support we need.

We need to feed our craft so it doesn't become stale.

But we also need to feed the beast.

Sure, back in the day, an author might have been able to write a book and be done with it. But that was before social media. Before digital changed publishing forever and forced authors to market their books direct to the consumer. It's not just the connection to the reader. If that were the case, discoverability wouldn't be so hard. But there's a lot of noise (competition) out there, and to reach readers with the right message isn't as easy as posting something about a book on any social media platform.

An author now has to really be savvy with their business. They have to understand things they never did before. They are taking courses in how to set up Amazon Ads, Facebook Ads, and dealing with other necessary marking avenues. It's not only about the writing anymore.

Though don't we all wish it were?

In 2010, I started a small digital company, Cool Gus Publishing, with *New York Times* bestselling author Bob Mayer. At the time it served as a vehicle to help Bob (and a few other authors) to get their backlist into digital, a medium that they had never been in before.

Here's another place I got lucky, because part of this business is all about luck. Or maybe it was Bob who got lucky since for the next seven years every time we went to a conference together everyone asked where could they find a "Jen."

The second component of this is being open to change.

Publishing stood at a standstill for years. It was business as usual until the Kindle came around and changed the game for all of us.

This is a good news, bad news situation. Good news: It opened the doors for talented authors who were being constantly rejected to finally have their books published. Authors who were given their rights back could republish their books in e-book for the very first time. Bad news: It also gave way to writers who published unedited and, frankly, unprofessional books. It made way for hackers who tried to game the system, making it harder and harder for legitimate writers to make a living.

The best piece of advice anyone has ever given me was to know I'm never going to be an expert at everything, but I better have a little more than basic working knowledge of the business I'm in.

As a writer, I need to work at crafting a better book every day. That's a given. Read books on craft. Take workshops. Discuss it with other authors. Read fiction! Stretch your writing as far as you can and then do it more.

Your readers will love you for it.

As an author, I need to strive to understand the business that surrounds me so that I can ensure that I'm making the best choices that meet my goals.

And that's key.

What are you goals?

Do you want to indie publish? Traditionally publish? Or both?

If you don't know the nuances of these choices and what they mean and what you as a career author will be required to do in each to be successful, then how can you achieve that goal?

Don't rush.

Publishing moves so fast now that we as writers often feel that we have to push so hard and quickly that we forget to take the time to consider everything that we are doing and if it's the right thing. We make decisions at the snap of a finger and then weeks or months later wonder if they were the right one. Or we go back and constantly change things, never giving anything a chance to stick.

Another piece of advice that has served me well is to be open to change because it's coming. I've had to reinvent myself three times. Not to mention the changing tides of publishing. I've had publishers go bankrupt. Publisher drop me. I've been a publisher. Kindle Worlds closed. Now I'm dabbling in putting some books in Apps.

But you can't do everything. You'll make yourself crazy.

That brings me to my final piece of advice: Be willing to take risks and try new things. Not everything is going to work, but you won't know unless you give it a go. I've had some ideas fall flat and others have taken off. If you're excited about it, try it.

One last word.

Write. It's what we do.

Jen Talty is the *USA Today* bestselling author of contemporary romance, romantic suspense, and paranormal romance. Regardless of the genre, her goal is to take you on a ride that will leave you floating under the sun with warmth in your heart. She writes stories about broken heroes and heroines who aren't necessarily looking for romance, but in the end, they find the kind of love books are written about. So, grab a glass of vino, kick back, relax, and let the romance roll in!

Read:
An Inconvenient Flame
https://books2read.com/u/m2eedk

Love in the Adirondacks—where hearts come together like the moon and the stars shining bright in the sky, showing the boats the way home at night.

The last thing she wanted was a man. But he was exactly what she needed.

Tayla Johnson doesn't have time for romance. She barely has time to stop and smell the roses. However, when her parents plan a big family reunion, she makes a promise to her mom and dad she will take two weeks off work and spend time with them and her two sisters. Something she hasn't done in years. She's ready for a little fun in her childhood home, but she's not prepared for the sexy next-door neighbor that won't take no for an answer. She doesn't want love or happily-ever-after. All she's ever known is work, career, and sheer determination.

Gael Waylen spent most of his twenties and thirties chasing dollar signs. He had no idea life had passed him by until his parents and baby sister were killed in a small plane crash six months ago. At their funeral, he vowed to make changes in his life, but he has no idea what that really looked like until the day Tayla Johnson came home. He sees in her exactly who he used to be and he doesn't want her to make the same mistakes. While he tells himself he's only trying to give her the gift of time, he ends up giving her his heart.

Amazon : amazon.com/author/jentalty

Bookbub: www.bookbub.com/authors/jen-talty

Facebook: the Talty Crew www.facebook.com/groups/191706547909047/

Goodreads: www.goodreads.com/author/show/2899568.Jen_Talty

Instagram: https://instagram.com/jen_talty

Twitter: https:/twitter.com/jentalty

Facebook Author: www.facebook.com/AuthorJenTalty/

Newsletter signup: https://dl.bookfunnel.com/od3icplesg

ONE OF THESE THINGS IS NOT LIKE THE OTHERS

Becca Syme

I'VE ALWAYS BEEN weird. Like, really weird. Some of you will identify hard with this—having been the odd one out or the kid on the fringes or the one no one understood. My people.

One of the benefits of being a writer is the ability (or the desire) to sink down deep into another person's head and tell a story from their point of view. Or to make one up. So, instinctively, I knew I wasn't wired like other people because I tried to write their motivations and emotions, which were so different from mine. Yet, somehow, I still held myself accountable to the standards of others.

I grew up in a disciplined household. Don't get me wrong—my parents are amazing, and they are my biggest supporters, and they are my two favorite people in the world. But both of them are extremely disciplined. They wake up early, they work out, they watch what they eat, they work the best when they really focus in and work hard. My sister is quite similar. Very dedicated. Focused. Driven.

And then there was me. Little Becca, living her best life, lying around on the deck reading books all summer instead of wanting to be out playing basketball and working out. Instead of running the gravel road in front of our house to get ready for athletics in the fall.

Of course, because my parents were happiest when they were disciplined, active, and focused, that's what I did. I played three sports most years, sometimes four. No matter how hard I worked, though, I was never as good as my sister—who had a natural ability for sports that I would just never have.

My first instinct was to let that stuff slide and just do what I was best at. Writing, music, singing, relationships, teaching, thinking. And while my parents were supportive, I always felt internally like there was something wrong with me. Something weird. Because I wasn't motivated the same as the people around me.

I wanted to be successful—a standout—at something. So I kept looking for the way to be more like the people I admired. My parents. My sister. Instead, I always felt weird. Different.

When I went to grad school for the second time, still casting around to find something I could be great at, part of the admissions process was doing psychometric evaluations. Personality tests, most of them. Names you'd be familiar with—a lot of people utilize them. And they were interesting. I'd done them before, most of them. But one test was just a little bit different.

I'd never heard of the "Strengthsfinder" (now called the CliftonStrengths® assessment, after the founder of the theory). So, being a naturally curious person, I was fascinated by the opportunity to talk to a professional coach about my results.

That one hour changed the entire course of my life.

Donald Clifton started his academic research with the premise of reality. Some people are more successful than others, in every single job. Everywhere you look, there are standout capacity people and then there are others who hit the "median" of behavior. He wanted to know why that was.

As it turned out: Our strongest behaviors pattern together (related traits forming neural nets that fire together) and when we spend time working in those strong behaviors, we get better, faster. Not just better, and not just faster, but exponentially both.

The early studies they did trying to isolate these behaviors (success patterns) led to one of my favorite studies ever. It was conducted to understand how much better students would get if they were naturally talented and had an amazing teacher. It was a speed reading study. The researchers put two groups of readers through the same speed reading class and studied the number of words per minute (wpm) they read.

One group was average (90 wpm) and one group was above average (started off at 350 wpm). Neither group had any training. After training, the average group stayed average (150 wpm). But the above-average group went from 350 to 3,000 wpm. (The world record, the last time I checked, was 25,000 wpm with 75 percent comprehension.)

That put them in the top of reading speeds. Standout capacity.

I didn't learn that in the "one hour that changed my life," but rather when I went to Gallup to get trained to be a Strengths coach a few months later. In the hour that changed my life, my coach operated on the assumption that standout traits were the shortcut to better and faster living, and he helped me to understand why what my parents had done never worked for me.

Their standout capacity was in being disciplined and focused and consistent.

That was the literal opposite of my standout capacity. Curiosity, creativity, unpredictability.

Here, my entire life, I'd been holding myself to standards that were hampering my abilities, rather than exercising them. Unintentionally— and this is zero shade on my parents. They supported me and loved me and gave me everything I ever needed, and more. But it was about me. Internally. I was holding myself to their standards.

When I look at my Top Five CliftonStrengths®, I see the five places where I have unlimited success potential. They are not the same as my parents. Or my sister. Or, really, anyone else I know. That instinctive feeling that I was strange ... the thing I'd always assumed about myself ... the weirdness. Turns out, that's not being weird.

Turns out, there is no "normal" behavior. Turns out, there are so many ways for us to be genuinely different (and successful, by the way—never forget that the Strengths were a study of success) that taking advice can be really problematic. Even when the people we're taking advice from are quite successful.

Because ultimately, what I learned about being "built different" is this: There really is no normal. There is no "industry standard."

In fact, in my work as an author success coach, I've studied the success patterns of so many authors (thousands and thousands by this point), I have yet to find one thing that all successful authors have in common.

Their speed, their planning, their intentionality, their creativity, their drive, their work ethic, their consistency ... *nothing is the same.*

When we were kids, many of us learned the "one of these things is not like the others" song as a way of learning how to tell what doesn't belong in a set. It's more of a math problem than anything else. But the true problem here is that "norming," or identifying a standard set of behavior, is destructive to success.

If you give me a set of blocks where all the blocks are square except one, and you ask me to pick "which one is not like the others," it might seem like helpful behavior. Now we can group like things.

Only … grouping "like" with "like" actually inhibits our success development in the long-term. It might make someone who grows up with very creative parents not want to go into the sciences because "that's not what we do." Or it might make someone who needs to think a lot before they write decide they're going to force themselves to write faster and stop thinking because "thinking is bad."

But some of us have an internal success pattern that revolves around thinking, which produces certainty. When you're wired to use thinking as a way to produce certainty, you need to think before you write. We call it being a "bread machine" writer. You take all the things from outside your head (research, experience, thoughts, ideas) and put them into the bread machine and let them cook. When they're done cooking, you can make a sandwich with it.

Have you ever tried to make a sandwich with part-cooked dough? It's awful.

Yet some of us are trying to make book sandwiches with part-cooked thought-dough because someone told us "you can't edit a blank page."

But … can't you? You tell me.

I've coached enough writers who are built like this to know, *yes, you can*. There are plenty of successful writers who function more like bread machines.

When I practice "norming" behavior, I'm actually sanding off the points of the star to try to make a "well-rounded" circle. If I try to "norm" a bread machine writer into being a faster writer, I might be knee-capping the very thing that could make them a standout writer.

After that initial hour of coaching, where I realized I wasn't "weird," just built different, my entire life changed. I started questioning the premise of any advice anyone told me because I'd seen just how damaging it could be, internally, trying to be something I'd never be. I was able to very quickly release the expectations that I "should" be successful in a way that anyone else was, and started studying my own success patterns.

My current ability to coach writers in their own standout success first began with me embracing my own. If I'd never released the expectations that I should be like others, I never would have found the success I've found. And that's really only modest success. Some of the authors I've had the privilege to work with have found such outstanding and incredible (six-, seven-, eight-figure) success because they have embraced their own individual process and allowed themselves to function in the way they're wired. Not because I coached them. Because they were aligned—sometimes even without me at all!

The one thing I'm glad I learned early, and the thing I wish I'd understood more at a young age, was that being built different matters. When we "one of these things is not like the others" ourselves, and we try to norm our behavior into a pattern that doesn't actually fit who we are, we keep ourselves from developing the Strengths we do have.

My hope, for all writers, is that we learn what to keep, what to quit, and what to question. Because everyone has advice for us (Becca, most of all), and everyone is trying to be helpful. But even the most helpful people (like my parents) can't change our wiring. They can't make us more like them.

There's good news, though. There is a way to achieve standout capacity for each of us. It's going to look different from everyone else. And it's going to take some releasing of the expectations we might have about what success "should" look like (*hello, bread machines!*). And it'll mean relinquishing the search for the silver bullet that will make me just like everyone else.

But it will be worth it.

Because being weird is a good thing. Weird is normal. Weird is success.

Becca Syme is a Gallup-Certified Strengths Coach with a Master's in Transformational Leadership. She's coached more than 5,700 individual authors in the better-faster methodology of success alignment. She is a *USA Today* bestselling author of romance, nonfiction, and mystery, and she lives in the mountains of Montana, where it is always winter and never Christmas.

Youtube Channel: www.youtube.com/ channel/UCqcMMgtLuogKNSbxlwyJ5ug

TikTok: www.tiktok.com/@becca_syme

Website: www.betterfasteracademy.com

Read:
Dear Writer, Are You Intuitive? (QuitBooks for Writers Book Book 6)

www.amazon.com/dp/B09WJ9V3JQ

FIND YOUR ISLAND

Melonie Johnson

THEY SAY BEING an author is a solitary profession, so perhaps it is ironic that what I feel has helped me most on my writing journey is my group of author friends. A support system of fellow writers to celebrate and commiserate, encourage and empathize, listen and advise.

No one else will understand the unique challenges you face like another writer. From writer's block and stressing about deadlines to juggling the demands of work and family, it helps me to know I'm not alone. It's not so much that misery loves company, but connecting to others who are dealing with the same things takes a bit of the pressure off.

And relieving that pressure is important. When we hang out with friends, we blow off steam and decompress. Spending time with author friends offers a chance to unpack our burdens and share writing woes with others who understand what we're going through. My group often refers to ourselves as an island,

and that is what we are—a place of refuge. We are a mix of writers of different backgrounds, at different stages in our publishing careers, but we've built a community of comfort and support. On our island, we muddle through our problems together, helping each other out.

Our island provides room to breathe. To think. To write. Sometimes it will be as simple as sharing how hard it is to carve out time alone. Airing out frustrations to my writer friends keeps me from stewing in a pot of resentment. We're all dealing with demands and distractions. We all have people in our lives—people we love—driving us bonkers. On our island, we rant about it, laugh and console each other, and occasionally even come up with solutions.

One such solution included "babysitting sessions," where two or more of us would get on a virtual call to write. We'd keep the cameras on and mics off, so we could see each other working. Yes, sometimes this level of accountability is necessary. Other times, organizing short writing sprints where we would check-in after twenty or thirty minutes was enough to boost productivity. There have been days we'd be moping about in the chat, complaining about all the work we had to do and how unmotivated we all felt, when one of us would declare that we should drop everything and spend the next half hour getting shit done.

Sometimes you need someone to give you that little push. To tell you to get to back to work, to finish edits, send that query, or follow up on a submission. Other times, you might need someone to tell you no. Wait. Maybe the work isn't ready yet. Having writer friends who care enough to be honest and tell you what you need to hear and not just what you want to hear is invaluable.

We all need someone in our corner to pull us back when something gets our hackles up, to take us aside and say, "Oh, honey, no." I'm sure you've seen it. A moment on social media when an author goes off. You wince and wonder, where were their people? Why didn't anyone stop them? Yes, we all need to vent about a mean review, bad cover, or whatever else is putting a bee in our bonnet. Tell your friends. Shout and rage and get it all out in a safe space. Relieve that pressure so you can breathe and think and focus on the writing again.

It's been more than 50 years since the Beatles first sang about getting by with a little help from their friends, but John and Paul knew what's up. I honestly don't think any of my books would have been written—or at least, probably never would have been finished—without my island of friends. Their support and encouragement has helped on every step of my publishing journey.

There's a common belief that success is about the people you know. Perhaps it is foolishly optimistic of me, but I believe that it's true, not in the conventional manner, but in a more idealistic sense. If I had to offer one piece of advice to other writers, it would be to find your island. Nurture relationships with author friends you trust. Surround yourself with people you respect and admire who respect and admire you. A circle of writers you call friends.

—

Melonie Johnson—#thewritinglush—is a *USA Today* bestselling author that enjoys sipping cocktails that start with the letter *m*. Declared a "writer to watch" by Kirkus and a "fizzy, engrossing new voice" by *Entertainment Weekly*, her smart funny contemporary romances include her upcoming romantic comedies, *Too Wrong to be Right*, the follow-up to *Too Good to Be Real* (a 2021 Buzzfeed and Goodreads pick for best romances of the summer), and *Too Wrong to be Right*, as well as her award-winning Sometimes in Love debut series: *Getting Hot with the Scot*, *Smitten by the Brit*, and *Once Upon a Bad Boy*. A former high school English and Theatre teacher, she spends her days in her Star Wars office, dreaming up meet-cutes. She lives in Chicagoland with her husband and their two redhead daughters.

Website: www.meloniejohnson.com/

Instagram: @thewritinglush www.instagram.com/thewritinglush/

Facebook Page: www.facebook.com/MelonieWrites

TikTok: www.tiktok.com/@thewritinglush

Twitter: @MelonieJohnson https://twitter.
com/MelonieJohnson

Read:
Too Wrong to Be Right
https://us.macmillan.com/
books/9781250768827/toowrongtoberight

A swoony, slow-burn rom-com, Melonie Johnson's Too Wrong to Be Right features a true romantic on a mission to find her happily ever after.

Release date: Feb 28, 2023
Pre-order available now:
https://us.macmillan.com/
books/9781250768827/toowrongtoberight

DEAR ASPIRING WRITER

Nina Crespo

WHAT ADVICE CAN I give you? I think the best way to start is by sharing my author journey.

A little over a decade ago, I was a solo entrepreneur in a different industry. My business advisor, who was also a friend, noticed that my interest in what I was doing had started to fade. She asked me if I had the chance to do something else, what would it be? I responded—I would be writing romance books.

This confession was just as surprising to me as it was to my friend. I loved reading romance novels but writing one had remained the thought hovering in the back of my mind that I always dismissed. But my wise friend wouldn't let it go. She asked, "Why aren't you doing that?"

I didn't have a good answer. I started writing the week after our conversation, and I haven't stopped.

Making the decision to become a writer was easy. The journey—it's been an eventful ride.

I've faced rejection and criticism. I've missed sleep over deadlines. I've flirted with imposter syndrome. I've indulged in wine, chocolate, and procrastination as coping mechanisms. I've wondered and worried over the smallest things, and as a result, stalled my creative process. But on the flipside of all that has been a really good time.

Completing a manuscript is exhilarating. Book release day arrives with a huge sense of accomplishment. Meeting wonderful readers and experiencing their enthusiasm has fueled some of my biggest smiles. The excitement of walking into a bookstore and seeing my book on the shelf will never grow old.

My happiness as a writer comes from the characters in my mind nudging me for a place on the page. I'm grateful to have more stories to tell.

It's important to know that the journey of an author is often filled with ups and downs as well as unexpected, and sometimes beautiful, twists and turns. Resilience is key. What else is needed along the way? I recommend the following:

A supportive network. When I need guidance, help with brainstorming or just an honest conversation about "author life," I turn to my accountability partner or writing coach and a few trusted author friends. They remind me I'm not alone in my fears or experiences. They're happy to celebrate my accomplishments, big and small. They understand the sweat and tears that go into every chosen word, and I love that I can support them in return.

Know your creative process. Lots of writing advice is available, and there are plenty of methods to choose from. If the latest and greatest technique doesn't work for you, don't consider that a failure. Keep the parts that work and set aside what doesn't. Your creative method will most likely be a mix of techniques you've learned along the way. It's about shaping them into an effective process that's the right fit for you.

Remember that distance is good. It's tempting to view always writing as the road to success, but it isn't. Fatigue and burnout are real. Creativity requires moments of rest to thrive, and you need time away from writing to engage with life. You are not *just* a writer. Rest, relax, take a pause. Trust me, you'll return to your computer mentally and physically in a better place.

And lastly, never forget why you became a writer. Let your joy as well as your words inspire your stories and fill the pages of your manuscript.

Wishing all the best,

Nina Crespo

Nina Crespo lives in Florida where she indulges in her favorite passions—the beach, a good glass of wine, date night with her own real-life hero, and dancing.

Her lifelong addiction to romance began in her teens while on a "borrowing spree" in her older sister's bedroom where she discovered her first romance novel.

Nina's sensual, award winning, contemporary stories satisfy a reader's craving for love, romance, and happily-ever-after. Her work has been published by Harlequin, Pocket Books, Kensington, and Entangled Publishing.

Website: www.ninacrespo.com/

Facebook: www.facebook.com/
AuthorNinaCrespo/

Instagram: www.instagram.com/
ninacrespowrites/

Read:
A Chef's Kiss, Small Town Secrets, Book 1
Buy: A Chef's Kiss - Nina Crespo

A welcome second chance...
Or a recipe for disaster?

After their ill-fated fling quashed her dreams, small-town chef Philippa Gayle's onetime rival-turned-lover Dominic Crawford upended her life. But when Philippa's forced together with the celebrity cook on a project that could change her life, there's no denying that the flames that were lit years ago were only banked, not extinguished. Can Philippa trust Dominic enough to let him in...or are they just cooking up another heartbreak?

TIPS, TRICKS, AND WRITING ADVICE

Emma Chase

WRITING IS MOST often a solitary activity. It is done on our own. In a room, or outside, or in a library; in the early morning hours or the long stretch of midday or the dead of night; at a desk or curled in a chair, probably while wearing noise-canceling headphones— we block out the existing world and create one of our own. Pulling our plots and characters from the confines of our minds and out onto the page. Giving the story shape and texture and infusing it with our soul, sweat, and tears.

Thoughtfully and carefully choosing 60,000 or 70,000 or 100,000 words to write is not easy. Creating characters that readers connect with and relate to on an emotional level can be draining. Composing snappy, smart, impassioned, and memorable dialogue that will touch the heart of whoever reads them can be intensive. In the homestretch to "The End," things get messy—there's stress and self-doubt, too much caffeine and not enough water, exhausted laughter, regrettable eating choices, and unwashed hair.

In the early days of my writing career, I believed these struggles were unique to me. That these were issues to be overcome and resolved. That I needed to try harder, work better, be more organized and more disciplined. But now I understand that these elements come with the writing territory. They are part of the creative process—part of the job.

One of the most wonderful things I've learned in my years as a romance author is that while the writing might be done by ourselves ... we are not alone. The idiosyncrasies, anxieties, habits (good and bad), the driving need to get a story down on paper and send it out into the world, and the blissful accomplishment, pride, and exuberance that accompanies the completion of that task is a shared experience for all writers.

Throughout my author journey, I've been lucky enough to receive advice from talented author friends and industry professionals, and learn valuable lessons from my own experiences. These bits of wisdom have helped me to become a better writer, a happier writer, who is more accepting and understanding of my writing process and the career I have joyfully signed up for. I hope they do the same for you.

No filter for first drafts.
A great deal of writing time can be wasted

debating the question, *Should I write this?* There's a voice in our heads that whispers, *That's a stupid line, a ridiculous plot point*—it's too unrealistic or too common. It's not good enough. My advice to you is: Write it anyway. Write it all, just as you see it in your mind. Don't self-edit your first draft, get the words down on the page. There have been lines in my books that were almost never written because I didn't think they were good enough for my editor to see. But I pushed myself to write them anyway—and they turned out to be some of my readers' favorites. We are our own worst critics, our biggest self-doubters. You can't revise a blank page and debating only whittles the time away. This is not your only chance, no first draft is written in stone—whether certain lines or words or plot points stay or go can always be worked out in the editing process.

This book should be burned.

I don't believe that reviews are meant for authors. They are not critiques that will improve your craft or that should be kept in your mind when you're working on your next project. Reviews are for readers. It's their reaction to a product, their opinions of a story that they are free to share. A bad review does not mean you are a bad writer, or that you should give up the pen and never write again (even if it actually says that). Don't allow yourself to be wounded or disheartened by a negative review. The truth is, some people are going to love your work and some really won't. That is how art—and opinions of art—work.

I understand this can be difficult, and there is a difference between knowing something logically and believing it. To internalize the concept, I suggest trying this: Find your favorite book (not one of your own) on a vendor or review site—the book that you believe is perfect and flawless and your forever go-to reread. And then read all the negative reviews that have been written about it. Next, find the book that you think is ... not so great. A story you didn't connect with or maybe thought wasn't particularly well-written. And read all the glowing five-star reviews from the readers who loved it. Doing this will help illustrate that reviews are a reflection of personal taste, expectations, mood, what has been read before, what will be read after, and a hundred other things you have no control over. You will never be able to please all readers and that should not be the goal. Instead, write what you love, write something you are proud of, and let that be enough to keep you going.

Writing a book ... how do you do that again?

Every time I start a new book I'm surprised by how hard it is. Even when it's a story I've been planning for months or years. Even when it's a story I've outlined, and story-boarded, and gleefully anticipated putting to paper. I laugh in comradery when I see a post from my author friends on social media that says, "Send help—I've forgotten how to write a book!"

When you've done something multiple times, it's supposed to get easier, right? Wrong. Writing is difficult—every time—if it wasn't, everyone would do it. So, if you find yourself beginning a new story but blanking on how this "book thing" is actually done, don't freak out. Keep going, keep moving forward, keep writing. I promise, somewhere along the line, you'll experience that infinitely comforting moment when you remember and say to yourself, "Oh yes! I do know how to do this!" And all will be right with the world again.

Speaking of "right" . . . if you haven't already, you will encounter a plethora of articles that purport to tell you the "right" way to write. They'll say that in order to be a "real author" you should write every single day, while other articles instruct to only write when inspiration strikes. You'll hear that you should write in the same place at the same time, and that you should write at different times, in different places. That you should write your book in order, that you should write out of order. That you must outline, or that you should just wing it and let the characters lead you where they will. That you should dictate your stories, or type, or write long-hand using a blue-ink ballpoint pen only. That you should write the story you want, that you should write the story that will sell.

Here's my take: The *right way* to write a book is any way that gets it written.

Trust *your* process—it is individual to you—your mind, your voice, your creativity.

True story: I write my books out of order. I wake up in the morning and work on the scene or chapter that is most clear in my mind at that particular moment. Sometimes it's chapter 17, sometimes it's the epilogue, sometimes it's a scene from the middle of chapter five. This method keeps me motivated and excited about the project and I find the words flow faster and better. After 15 full-length books, I know this is what works for me. And yet, every time I begin a new book, I spend the first week or so staring at a blank page, trying to begin at chapter one. Eventually, when that doesn't work, I jump to the scene that's already in my head, the one I can't wait to write—and it's a go from that point on.

I've come to accept that this delay is *also* part of my process. That for some intrinsic reason I have to attempt a method that won't work in order to move forward with the one that will. That during this time the story continues to percolate in my imagination—I think, daydream, and envision the scenes and settings, what my characters will say, how they'll move, what they'll think, how they'll feel. And that's perfectly okay ... because all of that is part of writing too.

Where oh where have my words gone?

It happens. You settle into your favorite writing chair, you have a glass of wine or coffee

by your side—maybe the fireplace is roaring—
and you are ready to create the next literary
wonder. And then ... nothing. Nothing but a
blank page, a blank mind, and a blinking cursor
silently mocking you. It's frustrating and scary.
When writing is a vital part of your life it can
be frightening to find yourself unable to do it.
We ask, often without answers, why this has
happened and more importantly, when things
will return to normal. I've found the best cure
for a lack of inspiration, a loss of "the words,"
or writer's block is to get out. Out of the house,
out of your shell, out of your own head. Go for
a walk, meet up with friends, hang out with
your children, play with your dog, visit your
parents, grab a bite to eat with your significant
other.

In our stories, we create new worlds and
the people in them—but that doesn't happen
in a vacuum. Sometimes you need outside
input to ignite the creative spark. Sometimes
you're just tired or drained and need to refill
the artistic tank. You can find inspiration at the
grocery store—at seeing a devilishly adorable
toddler running from a bleary-eyed parent,
or a handsome man in line at the coffee shop
texting on his phone, or a deeply in-love
PDA-ing couple oblivious to anything around
them, or an arguing couple glaring daggers at
one another, or a group of friends hugging
and laughing. A song on the radio, a flock of
birds, a lonely duck, rustling leaves, a car full
of teenagers. Inspiration is all around us, but at

times you have to go looking for it. Creativity is not an exact science, and in my experience no one involved in this profession expects it to be. Whatever your timeline or deadline, it's okay to put your project aside for a day or more, get out of your author space and just be a person for a while. The words will come back to you.

Stuck on you.
In every book I've written, there is one scene that likes to be difficult. One that, for a variety of reasons, just doesn't want to get written. I tend to save these moments for last and tackle them using a few different methods. If the trouble seems to be focused on how to begin—try starting with a straight line of dialogue. It's an active way of pulling the reader into the moment and propelling them forward to see who is speaking and why. If internal thoughts or descriptions are holding you up, write all the dialogue in the scene first, then go back and fill in the action and descriptions on the next pass.

If the entire scene has been written, but it's still not working, ask yourself if you are telling the scene from the right character's point-of-view or should the reader be seeing this moment through a different character's eyes? You can try writing the scene like an instruction manual (he said, she said, insert flap A into slot B), and revise it later with more elegant prose and vivid descriptors. Writing a character's stream of consciousness, even if it's random or doesn't make sense, can also be helpful. Focus on the senses—what are they seeing, feeling, hearing—what does the air smell like? Accept that this material will need to be revised and rewritten, that stubborn scenes may go through three or five or 12 versions—but sometimes we have to write something the wrong way in order to see *why* it's wrong.

Progress is the name of the game and moving forward, no matter how incrementally, is the challenge to be met. If you only get a handful of words that are keepers out of this process, that's more than you had yesterday, so that's a win.

The art of dictation.

One of the most universally liked and funniest scenes I've ever written is the Thanksgiving dinner scene in my first book, *Tangled*. The very first draft was written on a paper napkin in a McDonald's play room, while my kids crawled around in the jungle gym. Because that was the moment when the dialogue came to me and I had nothing else to write it down on (no, I don't still have that napkin; yes, I wish I still did).

Few things in a writer's life are more frustrating than coming up with a funny, or heart-wrenching, or stunningly beautiful line—a line that deserves to be embroidered and framed—and then forgetting what the actual line is. You know you had it and it was *awesome*, but you can't remember what it was.

The Notes app on your phone can be

effective in this situation in a pinch, but I've found good dictation software is worth the investment. Most versions are user friendly for even the least tech-savvy among us (raises hand) and over time the software can adapt to your style of speech for more accurate transcription. This is important because second only to the frustration of forgetting the perfect line is dictating it only to discover it's so mangled you have no clue what you were actually trying to say.

Dictating text can also be a time-saver. It's not an uncommon sight to find me pushing a shopping cart around my local grocery store with one hand and, with the other, speaking material into my phone that will be copy and pasted later into my manuscript. It's multi-tasking at its finest and there are times in life when multitasking can be a writer's very best friend.

Inconceivable!

Ah, the editing process. For most writers, editing is not their happy place. The very purpose of it is critical in nature and it can be difficult to accept critiques on your story, your vision, your book baby—no matter how gently its delivered.

Trust is vital. In order to be open to feedback on your manuscript, you have to trust that the individuals you are working with are professionals who understand your style and your literary voice, and that their goal is always creating the very best book possible. As the writer, you are inside the story. You hold in your mind features of your characters and elements of your plot that might not always make it onto the page. Your editor is looking at it from the outside—at the execution. It's crucial to bridge the story you want to tell, that you mean to tell, with the story you are actually telling.

In my experience, the most effective way to tackle edits is to read through all queries and feedback, revise the easy ones—and then walk away for a time. Take a breath, think about your editor's comments, and let the possibilities roll around in your mind. There have been times when, initially, I did not agree with my editor's suggestion. Moments when I said to myself (in Vizzini's voice from *The Princess Bride*, of course), "Inconceivable! I can't do that." Instances when I felt moving a scene, changing a chapter, deleting or expanding material would alter the pace of the story or the personality of a character too much. But by taking the time to contemplate, in more cases than not, I realized these revisions *were* doable—totally conceivable—and more importantly, that my book would be better for them.

It's time to celebrate.

It's easy to get bogged down by the pressure of writing—consumed by the to-do list and the deadline. But it's the wins in our writing journey that help keep us going and shore up the confidence in our own capability. Celebrate the good moments, big and small. Take note of every triumph, success, and milestone. Be glad, be proud. Relish the publishing contract, the self-published book birthday, the audiobook release, the completed chapter, the daily word count, the finished scene, the page, the paragraph, that incredible one line of dialogue you absolutely can't wait for your readers to see.

Never forget that this is your dream coming true. That you have accomplished what many never will—you are a writer. You put happiness out into the world and provide an escape from the burdens of everyday life. You are a weaver of tales, a spinner of stories, a designer of journeys, a composer of words, an invoker of emotions, a creator of worlds, and an architect of happy endings. Is there anything, anywhere, more magical than that?

Emma Chase is a *New York Times* and *USA Today* bestselling author of romance filled with humor, heat, and heart. Her books have been published in over 20 languages and optioned for film. *Tangled*, Emma's iconic enemies-to-lovers rom-com, was recently released by Passionflix and her royal romance, *Royally Screwed*, will be coming soon to the screen. Emma lives happily-ever-after in New Jersey with her husband, two children, and two adorable, misbehaving dogs.

Website: www.authoremmachase.com/

Facebook: www.facebook.com/
AuthorEmmaChase/

Instagram: www.instagram.com/
authoremmachase/

Twitter: https://twitter.com/emmachse

Read:
Royally Screwed

"Royalty is forever…"
https://authoremmachase.com/books/royally-
screwed/

THE POWER OF EDITS

Victoria Schade

L EAN INTO EDITS.
When I was working on my first book, I considered every word that I put on the page sacred. Even parts of the story that I knew in my gut weren't quite right had to remain because ... well, I wasn't exactly sure why I felt that way but I just couldn't bring myself to change anything.

When I finally landed my first agent, she had suggestions for how to improve the story, and while everything she said made sense, I still felt weird about making sweeping changes to a book that I adored.

Sure, she knew the industry way better than I did, but how in the world did she think cutting that super important part about the dog park was going to make the story better? And what about that one argument scene, did it really make my character seem unsympathetic? I was so besotted with the people and world I created that it turned out I was blind to the possibility that there were flaws in them. Of course, I didn't think it was a perfect book, but I wasn't completely open to the idea that improvements to it would require me to break out a hatchet and cut thousands of words.

Not exactly the right headspace for a collaborative relationship!

My "solution" was to implement my agent's suggestions but take those precious, discarded words and lovingly place them in a Word document for future use. I believed those passages were solid gold, so of course I was going to find a home for them at some point! The file grew swollen with stuff that I was convinced would be of use in a yet-unwritten book.

But guess what happened? I kept cutting (yes, it felt like I was murdering so many darlings) and pasting words into that document and ... never going back to them. The fact that the file remained untouched as I reached the midpoint of my second book made it clear to me that I didn't need those tossed-out words after all. And as I continued writing and editing, I eventually became bold enough to start killing words without any hope of resuscitation by simply ... hitting the delete key!

I finally figured out (late in the game) that no matter how dear I held my writing, there was always room for improvement. As time passed, I not only learned to lean into a scorched earth approach to edits, I came to truly love the process. Extra eyes on a manuscript, especially ones that know the business of books, only made my stories stronger.

I've reached the stage in my career where edits are one of my favorite parts of the book writing process.

Do they ever sting? Okay, maybe a teeny bit, but even if I'm cutting 30,000 words (yes, that's happened!) my finger goes right for the delete key without a moment of hesitation.

So lean into those red lines on the page without looking back (or putting them in a new document) because I promise you, your story will be that much better because of them!

Victoria Schade has been a dog trainer and writer for over 17 years. During that time, her dog duties have included working behind the scenes on Animal Planet's *Puppy Bowl* as the lead animal wrangler; appearing on two seasons of the Animal Planet show *Faithful Friends*; writing dog training content and appearing in educational videos for NBC/Universal, Pet360, PawCulture, and petMD; and writing two dog training books, *Bonding with your Dog* and *Secrets of a Dog Trainer*.

Victoria shares her 1850's always-in-need-of-renovations home with Millie the Smooth Brussels Griffon (who wants you to know that she is not a skinny pug), Olive the mixed breed dog, the occasional foster pup, and her incredibly tolerant husband, Tom.

Website: www.victoriaschade.com

Facebook: www.facebook.com/
VictoriaSchadeAuthor/

IG: victoria_schade

Twitter:VictoriaSchade

Excuses Are Well-Planned Lies: Write the Book

Erin Branscom

I'VE ALWAYS BEEN a story builder in my head. I've built complete towns, people, places, and fun stories that keep me entertained. I thought that was normal and everyone did that. I remember sitting with friends and telling them that was how I fell asleep at night: by updating my towns, people, and the funny things my characters were up to. That's when I realized that not everyone builds fake worlds in their heads. I would write these stories until they poured out of me into dozens of Word documents that are buried somewhere on my hard drive where they should probably remain forever. But I'd be lying if I said those Word documents didn't make me who I am today as a writer.

Life got busy and I worked, had four kids, and yet always still dreamed about writing. The truth of it is, I had no idea that someone like me could write books. Just a normal mom, someone who loved to voraciously read. I figured you had to have a fancy English or journalism degree to write books. That, my friend, is imposter syndrome at its finest. I don't know if anyone has ever told you this before and you fully understood it, but you can do whatever you're passionate about. If you can't stop thinking about it and if you want it bad enough, you can chase whatever it is with all you've got and you can do it. I am living proof.

In 2017, my family entered into a busy season with years of loss, heartache, and hardships. I lost my dad unexpectedly, when he was only 61, to heart disease and diabetes. Losing my dad broke something in me. Something that scared me and made me want to get my own health on track. I found out that writing clever and funny stories when your heart is broken is really hard. But writing can also be healing, too. My dad was a writer and I miss him very much. I wonder if he's watching down on me and proud of what I've become.

I didn't want to risk having the same fate as my dad, so I did a complete overhaul of my health. I lost 150 pounds on a very unexpected public journey on my YouTube channel, My Level 10 Life.

During that time I started writing my stories again. I didn't think they would go anywhere, but I couldn't stop writing. I felt like I needed to write like I needed to breathe. Little did I know that writing would save me in so many ways for the next few chapters of heartache that were railing towards me like a freight train.

My younger brother was murdered in October of 2020, the day before his 32nd birthday, by an impaired nurse who was driving to work in the morning with alcohol in her system. In the blink of an eye, he was just gone. The defense argued it was an accident. But when you have an empty container in your cup holder at 7:58 A.M. and get behind the wheel of a car, that's not an accident, it's a decision. The driver also had previous DUIs in other states. My brother left behind a six-month-old baby, Beckett, and a hole in our hearts that can never be repaired. The nurse who killed him got off with only 21 days of jail time. Anger never hit me so hard. I knew I needed to cope with this and eating my feelings and regaining my weight back wasn't the answer. So I wrote them. I poured my heart and soul into my books and did a lot of coaching and editing to get better at writing. I told my husband I didn't know where this was going to go but I was going. Writing saved me.

Fast forward to 2021, I was turning 40 and I decided I was going to go for it. It felt good to focus on stories instead of the heavy world around me and the anger at how messed up our justice system is and how it failed my brother.

I finished *Falling Inn Love*, which touches on drunk driving and how devastating that loss is. It's a very special book for me. I finished that one, and the second in the series poured out of me, and then the third. I wanted to write some stories that touched on some hard topics in life because, for anyone else out there who has been dealing with a broken heart or anything similar, I didn't want them to feel alone. It's hard to read books that are so positive when you feel like your world is shattered and the rug is iped out from underneath you.

We can either let the hard stuff break us or fuel us. I used my pain like jet fuel. I began pouring my pain into writing energy. Drafts and drafts of manuscripts stacked up on my computer. Imposter syndrome threatened to creep in, but I kept it at bay with daily persistence and consistency.

While I was writing on the side, I started hosting a show with Amazon Live called *Meet the Author Show*, where I interview authors and am able to sell their books directly on my podcast on the Amazon platform. I saw an opportunity to start something that nobody was doing and I went for it. I figured I could learn more about writing directly from the amazing authors of the books I loved reading. One of my favorite questions to ask the authors on the live show is, "What advice would you have for an aspiring author?" And the answers are everything. They are always so unique, beautiful, and encouraging that I kept thinking to myself, these should be in a book.

Fast forward to the winter of 2022, I had my friend and author Jennifer Probst on the show for the second time and told her my idea for putting the answers into a book and she loved it, too. She said she would love to co-author that with me. And that is how this book was born.

No matter where we are on this journey, we need all the steps—good and bad—to build us to where we want to be so that we can move forward and achieve our dreams when the timing is right. If there's one thing I've learned, it is that there is just no direct shot to publishing. It's a long and winding journey. But it starts with us. We have to believe in ourselves.

Whatever it is you have in the back of your mind that keeps creeping to the front and nudging you, listen to it. What would you do if you could do anything you truly deep down dream about doing? What would make you happy? Because if it's one thing that the last few years taught me, life can be short. We have to make the most of every single day and we owe it to ourselves to chase those hidden dreams.

Never give up and never let your past dictate your future. It's okay to grow, ebb and flow, and change. Without what we've been through, we can never become who we're truly meant to be. Keep chasing dreams, my friends!

Erin Branscom has read everything she can get her hands on for as long as she can remember. To this day, her favorite place is still the library. In 2021, after a decade of writing novels just for fun, she finally decided to finish a book series and has found writing novels to be her greatest escape. Erin is a passionate author's advocate and host of the highly popular *Meet the Author Show* podcast on Amazon Live, where she interviews authors live every week. She lives in Oklahoma, and loves traveling and spending time with her husband, four kids, and best friend Molly, a Boston Terrier mix.

Instagram: www.instagram.com/
mylevel10life/

Tiktok: www.tiktok.com/@mylevel10life

Facebook: www.facebook.com/
hellomylevel10life

Twitter: https://twitter.com/himylevel10life

EDITOR'S NOTE

ONCE AGAIN, WE both acknowledge writing a book is part of a bigger tribe, and many people have helped us get this book into readers hands.

Big thanks to Cris Freese, our editor who helped make this shine. Hang Le for the amazing cover design. Shauna, assistant extraordinaire, who organized and kept us on task, and our formatter, Jenn from Killion Publishing.

And finally, to each of the talented authors who donated their time and words to this project—thank you. This book was written and fueled by all of you. We'll be forever grateful.